SCRUM
FOR BEGINNER'S

The Best Guide Ever On The Market To
Learn SCRUM Step By Step

©Jym Lawrence

Table of Contents

Introduction

SRCUM FOR BEGINNER'S: The Best Guide Ever On The Market To Learn SCRUM Step By Step

There are several popular Agile processes such as Extreme Programming or XP, Scrum, pair programming, acceptance testing and feature driven development to name a few. Perhaps the most popular and widely used today is Scrum.

Scrum was formalized in 1993 by Ken Schwaber and Dr.Jeff Sutherland. Scrum has been successfully implemented at many top organizations round the globe such as Yahoo, Capital One, GE and Thoughtworks. So what exactly is Scrum, and how is it different from the many other methodologies or frameworks out there?

The word 'scrum' is derived from the game of rugby where a team collectively moves down the field to reach its goal. Scrum is an empirical process that encourages teams to challenge themselves a little more every time.

Scrum follows a process of 'Inspect' and 'Adapt'. Frequent inspection exposes issues or barriers and the team then adapts its approach as needed. This shorter feedback loop ensures that any product flaws are fixed early in the cycle.

Scrum is made up of certain roles, artifacts and time boxes. A Scrum team is made up of 5-7 people. Let us have a brief look at the various components of Scrum.

Scrum defines only three roles for its development team. These are the Product Owner, the Scrum Master and the Team. There is typically one Product Owner who serves as the customer or customer proxy and finalizes the requirements.

The main artifacts that are produced in Scrum are the Product Backlog, Sprint Backlog, Sprint Burndown and Release Burndown. Scrum introduces the concept of a time box. This means that a given event will have a fixed time and will expire at the end of the time limit. The various meetings in Scrum are allocated a timebox.

Scrum introduces the concept of 'done'. This is also called success criteria or acceptance criteria and outlines the conditions a particular feature must meet in order to be considered 'done' or complete.

The story board - used to portray the Sprint Backlog - is another mainstay of the Scrum process. This is a physical board in the team which could be part of a wall or several walls as needed. There is a concept of a 'story' which is a feature or high level requirement. Typically, any item from the product backlog could become one of many stories.

Scrum encourages collocating all the team members in an open group area minus walls. The idea is to encourage open communication and reduce overheads from emails or phone calls. Impromptu discussions between the customer and team members are pretty common in a Scrum room.

The Scrum artifacts are displayed throughout the area where the team sits and works. These include story boards, backlogs, burndown charts, barrier section, architecture maps, designs etc. The idea is that any relevant information should be easily visible to the team all the time.

This is informative as well as motivational. The information radiates or jumps out from all the charts and boards. Color coding is used to differentiate tasks, stories, barriers etc. A lot of software tools are available for tracking Scrum projects, but it cannot replace the effect physical information radiators have in my opinion.

Even though Scrum encourages collocation, it may not always be possible, especially in the case of distributed teams that are in multiple geographic locations. Scrum has been proven to be effective even in such situations and many teams practice distributed Scrum.

This is a high level introduction to Scrum. In this comprehensive GUIDE, I will be taking a closer and more detailed look at the various Scrum concepts.

Chapter 1

What Is Scrum?

Scrum is a simple project management framework for incremental product development that has become wildly popular in the software development community.

Usually paired with engineering practices from the eXtreme Programming (XP) community, Scrum is one exponent of the agile movement and represents a paradigmatic shift from "waterfall," a traditional project management approach that, until recently, has dominated software development.

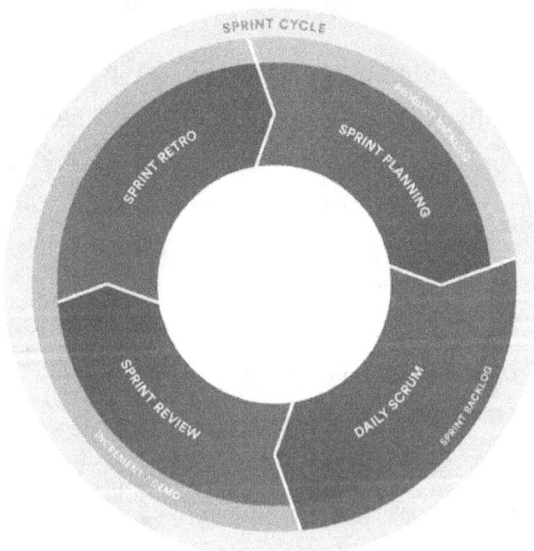

The Scrum method is deliberately designed as a framework-i.e., a lightweight management wrapper that can be applied to existing processes.

However, every part of Scrum's minimal framework is essential for realizing its core tenets of facilitating productivity through communication, collaboration, and self-organization. Given its spare structure, it's critical that all of Scrum's roles and processes are observed. Here's a quick overview of Scrum's primary roles and meetings.

The Scrum framework includes only three roles: The Product Owner, the Scrum team, and the ScrumMaster.

1. The Product Owner is the single individual responsible for the success of a project, which entails communicating product vision to team members and negotiating sprint goals with them.

As such, this person constantly reprioritizes the Product Backlog to reflect those items which will yield the highest business value. Because the Product Owner is responsible for generating a return on investment, this role possesses the authority to accept or reject each product increment at the sprint review meeting, which occurs at the conclusion of each sprint.

2. The Scrum team is a cross-functional and self-organizing team of about seven members (plus or minus two) that is responsible for delivering a functional product increment each sprint.

During the Sprint Planning meeting, the team negotiates the work it will tackle each sprint with the Product Owner and then, during the sprint, determines amongst its members how to complete that work.

3. The ScrumMaster facilitates team productivity and self-organization by removing impediments that obstruct progress, reminding all team members to observe Scrum's rules, and ensuring that all Scrum artifacts remain highly visible.

It is important to note that the ScrumMaster has no authority. This role functions as a servant-leader. Therefore, it is recommended that individuals who derive satisfaction from a team's success, not just individual heroics, are best suited for this position.

The Scrum framework includes four main meetings (Sprint Planning, the Daily Standup, Sprint Reviews, and the Sprint Retrospectives) as well as one important ancillary meeting Backlog Grooming.

1. During the Sprint Planning meeting, the Product Owner and the team negotiate the work that team members will attempt to complete in the next sprint. The Product Owner is responsible for identifying the highest priority work, while the team is responsible for committing to the amount of work it can accomplish within the confines of the sprint.

2. The Daily Standup meeting allows team members to deliver updates and exchange information on a daily basis. Every day, at the same time and place, team members spend fifteen minutes reporting to one another.

Each team member reports to the rest of the team what he or she did since the previous meeting, what will be done before the next one, and what impediments obstruct progress.

3. The Sprint Review meeting occurs at the end of each sprint. At this meeting, the team demonstrates the functional product increment it has developed and the Product Owner either accepts or rejects the work, based on the previously negotiated agreement.

This is an opportunity to "inspect and adapt"-that is, to examine the product's progress and revise direction, if necessary, for future sprints.

4. The Sprint Retrospective provides the team with an occasion to inspect and adapt its own processes. During this meeting, the team reflects upon its performance in the past sprint and brainstorms ways to improve going forward.

5. Backlog Grooming, which is known as the fifth Scrum meeting, creates a dedicated time for the Product Owner and team to come together to prepare the backlog prior to the Sprint Planning

meeting. Scrum literature recommends that teams spend five percent of their sprint on backlog grooming.

Although Scrum is a relatively skeletal framework, it is essential that practitioners acknowledge how purposeful its construction is. Each role of the framework is designed to create a balance-in terms of both authority and responsibility-for the members of a Scrum team, while Scrum's few meetings and artifacts sketch out necessary milestones within the development cycle.

Of course, there are ways that organizations can modify the framework to suit particular needs, but these basic aspects should remain intact and provide users with a roadmap for effective, continually improving product development and delivery.

Scrum is one of the simplest "agile" methodologies and is also proven to be highly effective for both software development and more general product development. Scrum is often used in financial product development.

Scrum is based on the idea that during a project the customers will almost certainly change their minds about what they want and need. To address this, a Scrum project moves forward in a series of short iterations each of which delivers an incremental set of improvements to the product.

Scrum has frequent intermediate deliveries with working functionality. This enables the customer to get a working product earlier and enables the project to change its requirements according to changing needs.

Scrum provides a set of practices and predefined roles which a team adopts in order to maximize the team's ability to deliver quickly and respond to changing and emerging requirements.

The Scrum team

A Scrum team is typically cross-functional and generally consist of around 5 - 9 people, however it can be much larger. The team has the responsibility to deliver the product. Scrum encourages co-location of all team members and verbal communication between team members.

A number of specific roles are defined in Scrum:

The ScrumMaster

Scrum projects are run using very flexible management style and require project managers with specific experience managing Agile projects. The project management role is non-traditional in that the ScrumMaster is primarily a facilitator who enforces the agreed rules, removes impediments to progress and ensures the team remains focused.

Scrum teams are self-organizing. The ScrumMaster is not the leader of the team and instead acts as a buffer between the team and any distracting influences.

Product Owner

The Product Owner represents the customer and ensures that the Scrum Team works on the "right things" from a business perspective. The Product Owner writes customer-centric "stories" which are one or two sentences in business language describing a specific product feature. These are then implemented by the Scrum team.

Stakeholders

These are the people for whom the project will produce the agreed-upon benefits. They are only directly involved in the process during reviews of progress.

"Sprints" and "Backlogs"

Work is packaged into small parcels of around two to four weeks in duration, called "Sprints". During each Sprint, the team creates a complete product increment resulting in a potentially shippable product.

The set of features that go into a Sprint come from a prioritized set of high level requirements of work to be done, known as the "product backlog". This product backlog contains broad descriptions of all required features for the new or enhanced product, prioritized in terms of their projected business value, along with estimates of the effort to deliver them.

Which specific backlog items go into a Sprint is determined during a planning meeting prior to the Sprint. During this meeting, the Product Owner informs the team of the items from the product backlog that they want completed. The team then determines how much of this they can commit to complete during the next Sprint, which becomes the "Sprint backlog" for the next Sprint.

During a Sprint, no one is allowed to change the Sprint backlog, which means that the requirements are frozen for that Sprint. After a Sprint is completed, the team demonstrates the product to the Product Owner.

The team can cancel a Sprint if they feel they are unable to meet the goals of the Sprint and external stakeholders can cancel a Sprint if external circumstances negate the value of proceeding. If a Sprint is abnormally terminated, the next step is to conduct a new Sprint planning meeting, where the reason for the termination is reviewed.

A publicly displayed chart is often used to show the remaining work for the current Sprint. This is known as a Sprint burn down chart and should be updated each day to provide visibility on progress. The transition from traditional methods of working to Scrum is relatively straightforward. You may benefit from engaging an experienced Scrum coach to assist in training and implementation.

Chapter 2

What Is The Scrum Methodology?

Scrum consists of self-organizing, cross-functional teams. Simply put, this means that the teams consist of a group of people who each have different areas of expertise but work together for the same outcome. A project manager does not control them, since their expertise empowers them to make decisions collectively.

The teams work in iterations, which allows the business the flexibility to change their requirements but still gives the development team the certainty it needs to deliver a working piece of the product. This is one key thing that makes scrum powerful.

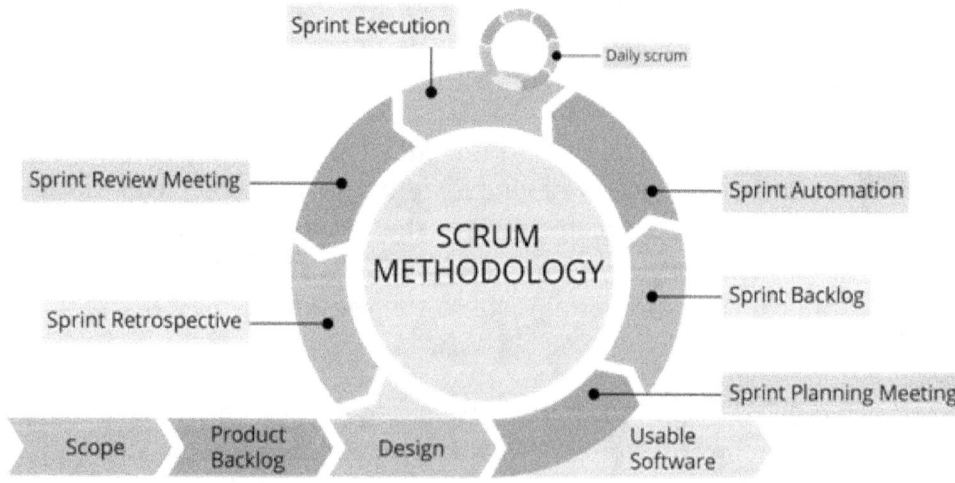

Scrum takes its name from the analogy to rugby where a team works together in a chaotic environment to keep control of a ball. This can be compared to a team working together in a chaotic environment to keep control of a project.

Scrum Theory

"History repeats itself, unless you do something about it!"

The framework is based on empirical process control theory. The idea is very simple so do not let the name worry you. It consists of three principles: transparency, inspection and adaptation. The idea is that the scrum team, agree to be transparent (honest) in all that they do on the project.

Being transparent means that functionality is not 'done' until it meets the development team's definition of done. Transparency builds trust between the team members. Once the team have agreed on transparency, they agree to consistently check up on progress (inspection) and make improvements based on what they have seen (adaptation).

These can be improvements in practices, sticking to values, communication or otherwise. This is powerful stuff in industry, the ability to consistently inspect and adapt. In that way they are improving time and time again before, during and after the release of a product. This is something that was not possible with the waterfall model of development.

Scrum Skeleton

The scrum skeleton is a very quick and easy way to explain the process to someone, so I will use it to explain the process to you.

We start with the product backlog, which is nothing more than a list of all the features (and their acceptance criteria) that the business desires for the product. A subset of that backlog, called the sprint backlog is taken on by the team, broken down into tasks, and worked on in an iteration called a sprint.

A sprint is a period of time less than thirty days in length and in that time, the team work on their tasks until they develop a working increment of the product.

Remember those mini phases of the waterfall I described earlier? Well this is where it all takes place. There is some requirements gathering and specification update before the sprint, then design, implementation and testing.

Above the large sprint circle, you will see a smaller circle. This represents the fact that every day the team meet to inspect on progress and adapt their plan for the day in a daily scrum meeting.

At the end of a sprint, the potentially shippable increment of the product is delivered. The business can review the increment in a sprint review and then release the new feature(s) to the world if they so wish.

The team then discuss (transparently) their progress during the sprint in a sprint retrospective (inspect) so they can improve (adapt) on things that need improvement or retain things that are going well. The cycle then begins again and repeats until the product owner has nothing more to add to the product backlog.

The scrum skeleton demonstrates the simplicity and power of scrum as a mini factory, churning out shippable features each sprint.

Teamwork and the idea of different parts working together in harmony to make up a whole are attributes valued by all companies. Because of that universally held ideology, Scrum was created.

Scrum is a very general, flexible working methodology, with the ability to be molded and sculpted to fit the needs of different teams, projects, and deliverable goals.

Scrum is loosely definable, adaptable best at an organization where goals are changing constantly and customers' needs greatly influence how the organization distributes tasks. In a nutshell, the Scrum methodology adapts to the ever-changing needs of customers and business, and that methodology is yours to do with what you wish.

Scrum breaks projects down into chunks called stories, allowing the development team to tackle each story as an independent project. The team works on these stories in set time increments, called sprints. For example, a team may be given a two-week sprint to work on a specific story, and a one-month sprint to work on the next, more challenging story.

One of the larger stories could be something like developing a new module for users to quickly find out which policies tie into which accreditation standard(s). A story with a smaller sprint could be something very simple, like having to correct a typo in a field title.

Every team needs a leader, and Scrum is no exception. With the Scrum methodology, a Product Owner leads the pack, and is responsible for writing stories and setting priorities.

The Product Owner creates storyboards with more detailed specs on a project. He or she also sets priorities on what order the team tackles stories in, as well as assigns specific story tasks to each team member.

Just like in sports, a development team thrives under encouragement and support. This is where the Scrum Master comes in. The Scrum Master is the equivalent of a sports-team coach.

He or she is part of the team, but also cheers its members on, helping the team deliver sprints on time and encouraging everyone to do their very best. The Scrum Master is also responsible for holding meetings to ensure the best quality work in the most efficient time bracket.

Why Scrum?

The Scrum methodology is used for many reasons. As mentioned previously, Scrum is flexible enough to be implemented within any organization and adaptable enough to fit any customer base, business needs, and the personalities, strengths, and project requirements of any development team.

As a result, the Scrum methodology makes a project completely developer-owned, allowing the team to take complete ownership and responsibility for all accomplishments and shortcomings.

This alleviates the sense of blending into the background that many employees may sometimes feel when working as a small fish in a big pond; with Scrum, this is impossible, because each developer has a specific task and everyone is working together to accomplish a solid common goal.

The Scrum methodology also helps alleviate stress in the workplace, because it breaks larger projects up into the aforementioned smaller, more manageable stories.

It allows the Product Owner to create a project backlog easily, and ensures team members are on the same page. The stories also allow for a large amount of flexibility.

For instance, if a customer has a problem with a specific portion of the product, team members can easily begin work on a new story that applies directly to the customer's issue instead of having to worry about many aspects of the project at once.

One of the best things about the Scrum methodology is that it doesn't apply only to software development - it is flexible and nimble enough to be used for any kind of task or project. For example, if you have to clean your house for a holiday party, your different rooms could be the project's stories.

As the parental figure, you'd be the product owner, writing and divvying up the different stories. The Scrum master (perhaps the eldest child) would be there helping with the current story (i.e. cleaning the kitchen), while at the same time encouraging his or her younger siblings to complete their sections of the story sprint on time (i.e. by the end of the afternoon).

Proud Scrumbuckets

The fact that there's an increasingly popular working methodology to make it simpler for companies to reach their customers makes it that much easier to uphold a family atmosphere and ensure clients are receiving the best quality service possible.

Companies grow and become better because of the Scrum methodology and passing on that knowledge with others will continue to encourage healthy team environments.

Chapter 3

Traditional Project Management Vs Scrum

Traditional IT project managers have struggled to use the PMI methodology when it comes to software development for decades. Using the traditional project management methodology for software development is similar to trying to put a square peg into a round hole; you can force it, but it just does not fit as well as it should.

Over the past several years, the Agile methodology has really started to gain momentum. This is in large part due to the popularity of Scrum, even though Agile has been around for nearly two decades. Scrum is one of several frameworks that fall under the Agile umbrella. Some of the others include Extreme Programming (XP), Rational Unified Process (RUP), and Design form Six Sigma.

Scrum vs. Traditional

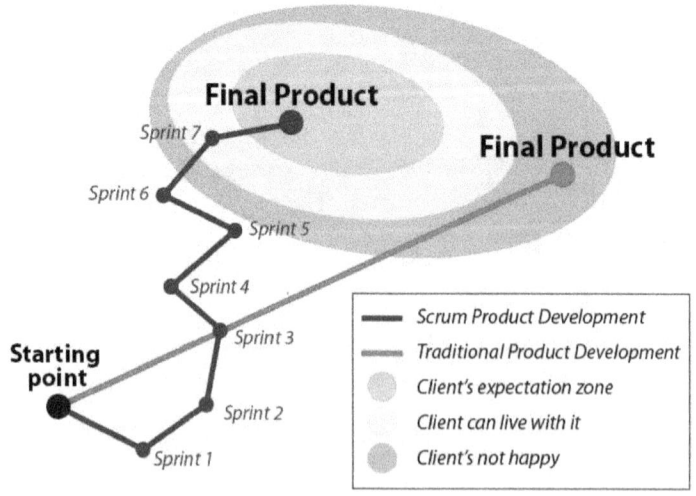

Control Theory

There are generally two different types of control theory. The first is the defined (or theoretical) process. This is what traditional project management follows; it's all about command and control. There are lots and lots of planning.

You plan what you expect to happen, then enforce the plan; sometimes regardless of the conditions. Finally, this process makes use of change control. You will often find a change control board that oversees any change requests.

Scrum, on the other hand, employs what is known as the empirical process. In this process, you learn as you proceed. Instead of planning everything up front and planning on how to handle change, the empirical process states to "plan for change." As a matter of fact, the empirical process embraces change through inspection and adaption; two of the three pillars that uphold every implementation of empirical process control.

The Three Pillars

Traditional project management for years has followed the "iron triangle"; time, cost, and quality. These are still the three pillars every project manager must juggle. In an ideal world, projects would be delivered on time, under budget, and be of the utmost quality. In reality, this rarely happens. For software development projects, obtaining all three never happens.

A ScrumMaster also follows three pillars. Their pillars are transparency, inspection, and adaption. Transparency involves open communication with all members of the Scrum project team, and the ScrumMaster proudly displays their team's burn-down charts where everyone can see.

They also review how well they did at during their sprint during what is known as a Sprint Review. Finally, adaption involves making changes and improvements to tasks that can be improved.

Beginning the Transition

For many companies trying to make the transition to Agile, the first thing they must understand is that a good project manager will not necessarily make a good ScrumMaster. They are not directly interchangeable. Contrary to some thought, a good ScrumMaster does not have to have Project Management experience.

As a matter of practice, the best ScrumMaster's are generally very technical. Former SME's and technical leads make for a great ScrumMaster. This is because they can better empathize with developers, they understand the big difference between level of effort (LOE) and duration, and they can better help prioritize features along with the Product Owner.

Know Your Role

There are three primary roles in Scrum: the ScrumMaster, the Product Owner, and the Team. Oftentimes, you'll hear people being referred to as "chickens" or "pigs". People who make up any of the three primary roles are referred to as "pigs", while everyone else is referred to as "chickens". A "pig" is someone who is committed to the project, whereas a "chicken" is someone who simply involved.

The origin of these terms comes from the following story:

"A chicken and a pig are together when the chicken says, "Let's start a restaurant!" The pig thinks it over and says, "What would we call this restaurant?" The chicken says, "Ham n' Eggs!" The pig says, "No thanks, I'd be committed, but you'd only be involved!"

ScrumMaster

The ScrumMaster's primary job is to adhere to Scrum values, practices and rules. They are an advocate for Scrum and help it get accepted and adopted throughout the organization. They also act as the figurative "shield".

The ScrumMaster protects the Team from outside political noise and ensures nobody goes directly to any team member without following the proper chain-of-command.

This allows the team to remain focused on the job at hand, and if any issue is a priority, the ScrumMaster and Product Owner will discuss it and prioritize it within the Product Backlog as appropriate.

Product Owner

The Product Owner's primary responsibility is to manage the Product Backlog. The Product Owner is a single person, not a committee. The collection of stakeholders can influence the Product Owner, but the Product Owner has the final say. The Product Owner sets the priority of each feature/request. For new Product Owners, the ScrumMaster will work closely to teach him or her how to do their job.

The Team

The Team is responsible for turning items on the Product Backlog into potentially shippable functionality every Sprint. The Scrum Team is cross-functional. In other words, they consist of people with one or more specialties; including, but not limited to quality control, development, data base design, business analysis. The team is self-organizing and self-managing. As such, everyone has the same title: Scrum Team Member.

The team size should be around seven (7) people, plus or minus 2. This size does not include the ScrumMaster and Product Owner (unless they are pigs who work on tasks included in the Sprint Backlog).

Transition Hurdles

Agile Methodology does not conform to PMI Methodology. This is absolutely the largest hurdle to overcome and where the internal conflict of project managers occurs; even more so for seasoned

PMP's. To successfully complete the transition, the department must choose one or the other when it comes to Software Development. Failure to conform to the Agile principles will lead to a failed transition.

Dual Role or Two Different Resources

Any transition to Agile is in-and-of-itself a project. Therefore, a Project Manager should be chosen to lead this transition. Also, the ScrumMaster's lifecycle is revolved around software development; which is only a subset of the entire project lifecycle.

As any Project Manager is aware, being a Project Manager is a full-time job. Being a ScrumMaster is also a full-time job. The big question is can a single resource successfully perform both roles? The answer, like so many requirements developers are given is, "it depends."

Some companies will try to fill both of these positions with a single resource due to budget constraints or other reasons. This is a perfectly acceptable reason, but not necessarily the best one. A Project Manager who is a Certified ScrumMaster can perform this dual role, but this is discouraged.

Deprograming Project Managers

Traditional plan-driven project managers must be deprogrammed before one they can become a successful agile project manager. President Eisenhower said it best when he said, "Planning is essential, plans are useless."

That phrase sums up the biggest difference between Agile and PMI. Success is no longer measured by how well the triple-constraints are balanced; it is only measured by the Customer.

Project scope is no longer the driver; scope is driven by time and budget. No longer is success measured by the completion of tasks and phase-gate reviews it is measured by the delivery of features and functions. Finally, learn to embrace change; love it, live for it.

Working Together

The Project Manager and ScrumMaster must be treated as peers if the project is to be successful. The Project Manager is in charge of the entire project, whereas the ScrumMaster is in charge of the software development portion of the project. It is very important that Management respect the difference.

During the actual software development, the project manager must let the ScrumMaster run Scrum using the Agile methodology, not the PMI methodology. As a Project Manager, the tricky part is "letting go" and trusting the ScrumMaster. This portion of the EXECUTE process group must be considered a "black box". The Project Manager is now considered a "chicken"; he or she can listen in, but carries no weight.

Becoming Truly Agile

Many companies feel they are Agile simply because they are doing iterative software development. However, doing Waterfall in an iterative fashion is definitely not Agile. Agile is much more than iterative development and rapid releases.

The traditional PMI way of thinking cannot be the guide while implementing Agile; it will become an impediment. It is a whole new way of thinking; a whole new philosophy. To become truly agile, the entire IT department must go through a paradigm shift.

Chapter 4

Why Scrum Works

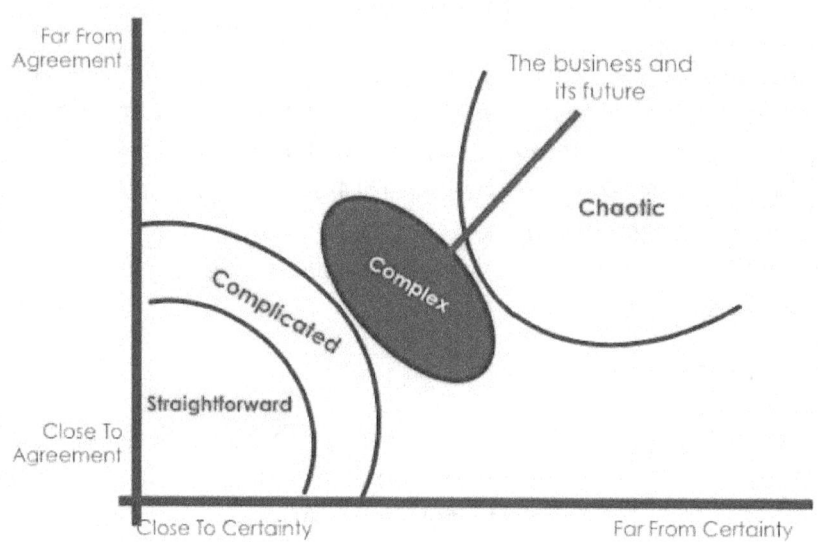

Reasons Why THE SCRUM MASTER ROLE Works

1. Dedicated bulldozer: Unlike other frameworks, the role focuses one person on removing obstacles. This means that the team can concentrate on getting the job done.

2. Dedicated coach: The role gives one-person responsibility for coaching others. No one can "pass the buck" on this. Therefore, one person has the focus of helping all members of the organization to understand the framework.

3. Impartiality: A scrum master can be as helpful to a team as a product owner (see below) without picking sides. The only focus is on making sure the framework and project is successful. This can help solve problems and gain trust.

4. Responsibility for framework not delivery: This is almost reverse psychology. The scrum master is only concerned with making sure the framework is carried out as the scrum rules say.

Divorcing the responsibility for the framework from the responsibility to deliver means that he or she can concentrate on making sure that rules are followed which in turn creates a well-oiled machine. If the scrum master's job is done and everyone in the scrum team is performing their role, then the development team can deliver.

5. No single point of control that could fail: Since a scrum master does not control the team, the absence of one does not leave the team in disarray. The scrum master sets up a system that everyone can follow in his or her absence.

Reasons Why THE PRODUCT OWNER ROLE Works

1. Time maximized for business return on investment: The product owner is not responsible for delivering the work or maintaining the process but simply for making priority calls and maintaining the requirements backlog. This allows a great deal of focus.

2. Dedicated source of requirements: There is no one else in the organization that needs to be consulted on a project's requirements. Senior stakeholder requirements flow through the product owner for a single point of contact.

3. One person responsible for changes in requirements: As the business picture changes only one person needs to capture the new requirements and update them.

4. Achieves the best compromise: Even senior stakeholders will need to trust their product owner with the final decision. This aligns the business and makes appropriate compromises for the good of the product.

5. Aligns the customer and team, daily: This role is the interface between the business and the team. His or her presence at all the scrum meetings means that the team is always acting on the latest information.

Reasons Why The Development Team Role Works

1. A group of dedicated experts: Explicitly calling the team out as experts, means that scrum teams are assembled to solve problems on their own. This frees up other roles to focus on their own areas of expertise.

2. Flexible to business needs: Scrum teams adapt to a given situation in order to get a product increment built. Any decisions should be tied only to a business requirement. This in turn gives a business long and short-term flexibility and reduces wasted effort in favor of targeted effort.

3. Lean and cost effective: The small size combined with high degree of expertise means that things get done to a high degree of quality with minimal technical communication.

4. Less management needed: Teams organize themselves. This means that everyone else can concentrate on his or her own role.

5. Highly scalable when given the resource: Large teams can be separated and organized through regular meetings called scrum-of-scrums. The teams each have scrum masters to keep them coordinated. Caveat - when two or more teams work on the same code-base, the team will need to decide if this is feasible.

Chapter 5

The Daily Scrum

The Daily Scrum or Daily Standup is an integral part of the Scrum process. It allows the Scrum team to 'inspect and adapt' on a daily basis and exposes any barriers or obstacles the team may face.

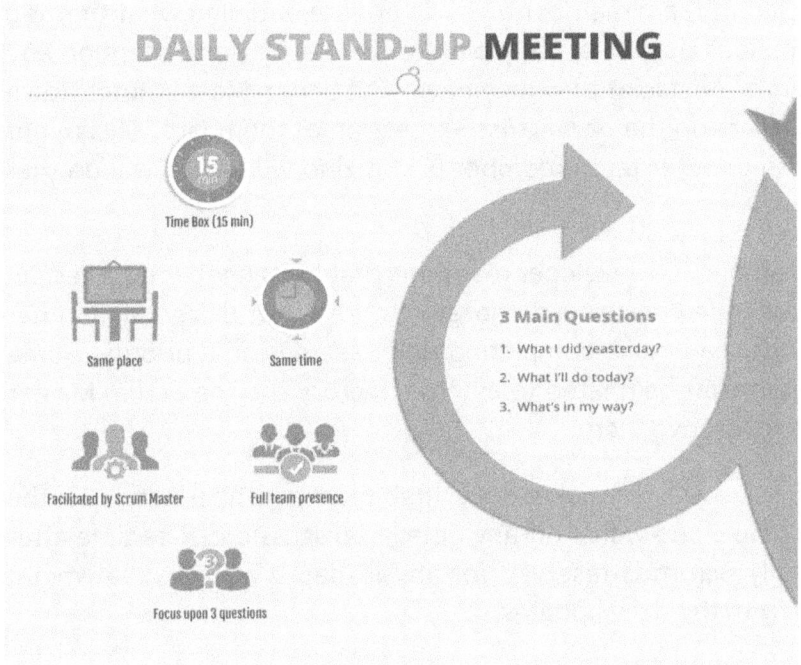

This is a time boxed event limited to fifteen minutes. The Scrum Master conducts the Daily Scrum and makes sure that team members stick to the agenda and that the meeting does not go over fifteen minutes.

Time, place, duration

The Daily Scrum is held at the same place and time every day. This makes it easier for everyone to remember and mark their calendar. Team members are expected to be punctual and be there for the entire fifteen minutes. Many teams encourage attendance by enforcing some fun penalties on slackers. The team stands in a circle while discussing the prior day's events.

The Daily Update

Each Scrum team member gives an update outlining what they did the previous day, what they plan to do that day and mention any barriers or obstacles they may have. The Scrum Master notes down the barriers on the barriers/issues section of the board. This might result in another team member prioritizing what they will do that day.

For Example, if a developer mentions that he cannot write a certain piece of code because a database feature is not designed, another developer can make completing database design a priority. Some barriers might be related to external factors and the Scrum Master works to remove them.

The Scrum Master makes sure that team members stick to the three points and wards off any detailed discussions. The time after the Daily Scrum is reserved for any in-depth analysis that might result from the daily updates.

Updating the Backlog

The Daily Scrum is also used to update the Sprint Backlog. Although some teams may use online tools to maintain the Sprint Backlog, this is still an effective visual aid. Team members move the cards that they have finished to the 'Completed' section, or reduce the effort remaining for any particular task to reflect the work done.

This gives the team members a sense of satisfaction about work they completed and is encouraged. At the end of the Scrum, the Scrum Master counts the remaining hours on the Sprint Backlog and updates the Sprint Burndown Chart accordingly.

The updated burndown chart gives the team an indication of their progress. It is possible to have a flat line or an upward line, and this will indicate that things are not going as planned.

Distributed Scrum teams also need to have the Daily Scrum. If only one or two members are in a remote location, they can dial in or email their updates to the Scrum Master. The Scrum Master will let the team have these updates during the Scrum.

If there are more people in each location, everyone can have their own Scrum and just send the updates to the Scrum Master. Technological gadgets also aid remote teams making it easy to have video conferences using Skype and similar tools.

The Daily Scrum is meant to encourage open communication between the team members. The team members should feel comfortable to give honest updates even when they were not able to achieve what they planned.

The heart of the Scrum process is embodied in the daily standup meeting, also commonly known as the daily Scrum, which emphasizes Scrum's tenets of communication and transparency. This meeting is critical to ensuring that every member of a development team is on the same page.

Each day, a Scrum team gathers in a predetermined spot-a team room or office-to update one another on the progress made since the last meeting, what they will attempt to do before the next one, and any impediments standing in their way. These updates are commonly phrased as responses to the following three questions:

• What have I done since the last Scrum meeting (yesterday)?

• What will I do before the next Scrum meeting (tomorrow)?

• What prevents me from performing my work as efficiently as possible?

This meeting is usually time-boxed to 15 minutes. If team members need to discuss an issue that will require more time, it is recommended that the relevant individuals involved meet in a "sidebar" meeting immediately after. This way, team members only attend meetings that directly involve their work, while others can get back to work.

Unfortunately, there is a tendency for daily Scrums to go longer than 15 minutes. To compensate, many teams use stop watches or timers to uphold the time limitations.

To cut down on extraneous small talk, some teams also employ a talking stick or mascot, in which the team member holding the stick or mascot is the only one permitted to talk. When he or she finishes his or her update, the talking stick or mascot is passed to the next team member, who reports, and so on.

When the daily Scrum meeting occurs is something for the team and Product Owner to determine, but, most Scrum literature advocates holding the meeting early on in the day - usually, as soon as all the team members arrive in the morning.

The daily standup is one of the most important processes in the Scrum method of agile software development because it formalizes communication and impediment resolution.

Flexible Approach to Daily Scrums

I see daily stand-up meetings ("daily scrums") as a one of the most beneficial practices in SCRUM's repertory. Theory says that during the daily scrum each team member should answer three well-known questions:

What did you do yesterday?

What will you do today?

Are there any impediments in your way?

Daily scrum is a great example of small things which make great difference. Three simple answers from each team member ensure that entire team is on the same page. It's clear who is working on what, what will be achieved by the end of day, what problems we have etc.

What I find strange is that theory doesn't leave much room for any discussion during the stand-ups. Discussions should take place during the follow-up meetings, immediately after the daily scrum. In general I agree with this rule. Bigger issues which don't require entire team can be talked through later.

But I think it's much more beneficial for a team if all members are allowed to jump in anytime during the daily scrum to add anything they find helpful. I have seen many scenarios where such impulsive hints work very well.

Although scrummaster has a tough task with keeping the discussion under control. On the other hand the worst thing which can happen is when team members are in 'on hold' state until it's their time to speak. That kills spontaneous knowledge sharing and potentially turns daily scrum into a progress report with limited profit for a team.

It's vital however to keep the meeting under 15 minutes and stay high level. There is not enough time for the team to go into each and every detail. That should happen during the follow-up meetings. Scrummaster responsibility is to ensure that discussions are on reasonable level.

Chapter 6

Scrum Product Backlog Grooming

Although the scrum product backlog grooming (or maintenance) meeting is not a formal part of the Scrum process, Scrum's founder Ken Schwaber nonetheless advises that teams dedicate five percent of its time, per sprint, to this activity. (As with Scrum's other meetings, it's recommended that the scrum product backlog grooming take place at the same time and place and for the same duration each sprint.)

The backlog grooming meeting is attended by the team, the Product Owner, and the ScrumMaster. During the meeting, everyone works together to prepare the backlog for the next sprint planning meeting. This might include adding new stories and epics, extracting stories from existing epics, and estimating effort for existing stories. Why do this?

Because a well maintained backlog will prevent sprint planning meetings from lasting an unnecessarily long time. If scrum product backlog items are written with clearly defined acceptance criteria and estimated by the appropriate team members, the planning process won't be stalled with work that could have been accomplished prior to meeting.

Dedicating a time each sprint to scrum product backlog maintenance ensures that this preliminary planning always occurs. It also renders lengthy, even tense conversations about estimation, prioritization, etc. irrelevant.

In all, scrum product backlog grooming offers a project team a chance to discuss stories and modify them in advance of the planning meeting. It might be hard for a team to pull away from its work mid-sprint, but this preventative maintenance will help keep your sprint planning meetings productive and to-the-point.

In the Scrum method of agile software development the single most important artifact is the product backlog. The product backlog is a list of all the requirements necessary for a system, project, or product.

In essence, it is a comprehensive to do list, prioritized by the business value each piece of work will generate. But from a philosophical standpoint, the scrum backlog is what drives the business-by breaking down the big-picture story into manageable increments of work called Product Backlog Items (PBIs).

During the sprint planning meeting, the Scrum team negotiates with the Product Owner about what work they will take on during the next iteration. At this point, the Product Owner moves PBIs from the product backlog (basically, everything the company needs to do) into the sprint backlog, which is limited to the work to be completed in the next iteration.

So what does a product backlog look like?

That depends on whether a Scrum team uses manual agile or an agile tool to monitor development progress. With manual agile, a team would create a list of its backlog items on a dry erase board,

Post It notes, or a taskboard. This works great for teams who all work in the same office or room because every team member can easily consult the product backlog, the sprint backlog, and the status of its stories.

When Scrum teams are geographically dispersed, however, they often require a tool to help them manage their agile software development. There are a number of tools on the market designed to bring un-collocated teams together with a virtual taskboard.

Such tools also offers deeper, more detailed views of the product and sprint backlogs, organized in adjacent panes and easily modified with drag-and-drop prioritization.

Although the team is responsible for completing the work, only the Product Owner can prioritize work in the scrum backlog or, with the team's consent, add work to the sprint backlog.

Be sure to check out a scrum software tool and scrum master certification classes

The Purpose And Goals Of Carrying Out Product Backlog Refinement In Scrum

The official scrum guide mentions about carrying out routine maintenance activities to update the product backlog, or to carry out the product backlog refinement. The exact time to be invested in the grooming activity depends upon the management, and how scrum is to be implemented in the project.

A rule-of-the-thumb followed is to put in approximately 10% of the time utilized during the sprint activity, into the grooming activity. It is important to be clear regarding some of the aspects associated with product backlog refinement.

Purpose and goals of carrying out the refinement

The primary reason why the product backlog should be refined is to update or rebuild the backlog so that it remains consistent with the requirements provided by the stakeholders with regards the new features and functionality to be included in the project.

Another reason is to review existing user stories or product backlog items and decide whether they are still useful or pertinent from the development point of view, and to update the acceptance criterion and the explanation detailed in each PBI.

It is recommended to use the "DEEP" method - detailed appropriately, estimated, emergent, and properly ordered - while prioritizing the user stories within the backlog.

Larger stories or epics should be systematically broken down in to more manageable smaller ones, proper estimation by assigning relevant story points to the PBIs should be carried out, user stories should be rearranged as per the new priorities, and the queries regarding the development of user stories during the sprint should be effectively answered by the product owner.

Whenever a meeting is planned to refine the PBIs, the objective should be to carry out enough refinement work so that it lasts for at least three future sprints.

Duration and frequency of the grooming activity

Each activity and meeting is time boxed in scrum. Following the same principle, the product backlog refining or grooming activity should be time boxed too.

However, in practice, there is no pre-designated activity or a meeting for planning and carrying out the product backlog refinement activity in the same manner as the sprint planning meeting and the sprint retrospective meeting is held.

Backlog grooming is carried out more as a routine activity than anything else in scrum, and the guide does not exactly specify how much time or efforts should be invested in the activity.

Perhaps a possible reason could be that the product development and creation of product backlogs vary from project to project, and it is difficult to standardize how the grooming activity should be carried out since the size and nature of the product backlog cannot be adjudged.

In practice, ideally time equivalent to 10% of the total time spent during the sprint activity should be allotted for the product refinement. For a two week sprint consisting of a total of 6 working hours per day and 14 sprint days per sprint, the time to be allotted should be approximately 10% of 6 hours x 14 days = 8.4 hours (10% of 6 hours x 14 days = 84 hours).

This could be rounded up to one working day. Since the refinement activity is to be carried out on a consistent basis, investing additional time could lead to decreased productivity and an extended product release date - something that should be avoided. In actual practice, this rule suffices to a great extent.

Who should participate in the grooming activity?

Besides the product owner, the grooming sessions should be attended by the development team members and the scrum master. The stakeholders can participate in the sessions too, but their participation should be a passive one, and they should not volunteer opinions, or try to disturb the sessions in any way or manner. Moreover, the product owner should try to limit their numbers during the sessions so it does not become overcrowded and difficult to hold the meeting.

Maintaining a proper approach

It is important to remain focused, and the product owner should be clear whether a particular product backlog item should be estimated again, or it ought to be detailed in greater depth, and additional explanation provided regarding its acceptance criteria.

The team members should remain focused upon understanding the PBIs and if required they should demand explanations regarding the acceptance criteria and how the development should be carried out during the sprint activity.

Chapter 7

The Product Owner In Scrum

A team practicing Scrum has three pivotal roles - the Scrum Master, the Product Owner or PO and the Team. The Product Owner is an integral part of a Scrum team. He is the guiding force that helps the team realize the product vision. A fully engaged collaborative PO is essential for a Scrum team to be successful.

The Product Owner is the product manager who has intimate information about the product. He acts as the customer proxy and is closely associated with the product vision.

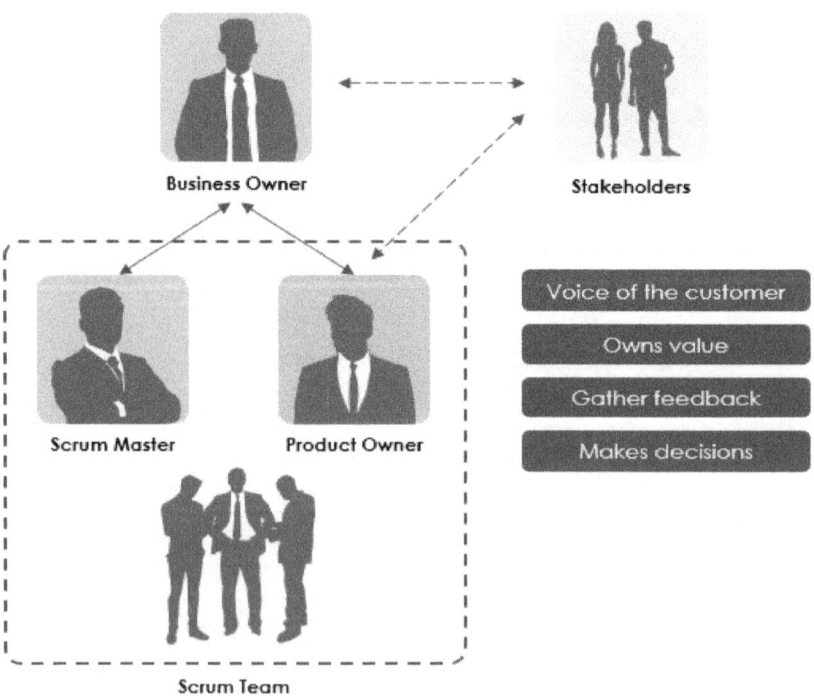

At any given point of time, he should be able to point out the features that are most important for the product, and should assist the team in building these highest value features early on.

One of the advantages of Scrum is that the highest value/ most important parts are built first and are ready for release. The Product Owner's contribution is essential to realize this.

The Product Owner assumes ultimate responsibility for the success or failure of a Scrum team. He is charged with the task of realizing the maximum ROI or return on investment.

What makes a great Product Owner? Apart from detailed product knowledge, what does the Product Owner need to drive a Scrum team to success?

Here are a few traits that I feel are important to be an effective Product Owner:

Total Commitment - complete engagement with the Scrum team is essential. While it may not be possible to be physically present in a Scrum team room all the time, the PO should be available via email, social media, messenger etc. The idea is to appear approachable so that the team members do not hesitate to voice their questions.

Product Backlog owner - the PO owns the Product Backlog. This is an ordered list of all the features that are desirable in the product. The PO continuously orders this according to changing business priorities and must be on hand to answer any questions regarding the backlog.

Subject Matter Expert - As an expert who should know the business and the product inside out, the PO is the go-to person for the Scrum team to answer any product related questions.

He is the sole authority on the product and must be able to explain any business logic or detailed functionality that needs to be built in, and thus should assist the team as they work on their Sprint tasks.

Collaborative - Being collaborative and a good communicator is essential for the PO. He should be able to place himself 'at par' with the Scrum team and be open to deal with them at a peer level.

A change in mindset might be needed here! Even though the person who is the PO is much higher in the organizational hierarchy, he/she needs to blend into the team and work shoulder to shoulder to achieve the common goal.

Scrum Product Owner's Role

Agile professionals have often discussed what the exact role of a product owner should be in Scrum. What virtues should a product owner possess to be considered a "good" PO? The answers are many.

And this is not surprising because Scrum is a framework, and its implementation in a project depends upon the requirements specific to the project. When requirements change, the role of the PO also changes. Therefore, it may not be possible to standardize the exact role a PO should play in a Scrum project.

A certain process flow remains common to almost all Scrum projects. The role of a product owner can be thought about in terms of what POs actually do in a typical Scrum project. Here are a few suggestions:

Common role or activities of a Scrum product owner

• Creating the product backlog as per the product vision seen by the stakeholders. Defining user stories having high business values in the backlog so the project "value" is constantly maintained.

• Monitoring and tracking all Scrum activities. The role of a product owner may be difficult to act since a project might be demanding, and the product owner may have to cater to market related issues and still monitor the work carried out by the team. Balancing both the aspects can prove to be trying.

• Make sure that the product backlog is kept refined at all times. Moreover, the product backlog should be accessible by the entire team.

• Each product backlog item "PBI" should be properly stated and defined in the product backlog. The story description, appropriate business value, and the acceptance criteria should be stated precisely in the story card and explained to the entire team so the team members can develop effective stories and develop shippable product features.

• To be available whenever needed, to remain present, and share information, knowledge, as well as expertise with other team members.

• The PO responsibility should also include defining productive sprint goals just before a sprint commences.

• A product owner's responsibility should also include respecting and aiding everyone involved with the project and ensure the project is completed successfully.

• Not try to influence the mind-set, or psyche of the team members regarding any issues and encourage the team to get involved in the project to achieve better productivity.

The role of a product owner can be a difficult one to play. Since the PO owns the project on behalf of the stakeholders, he/she has certain responsibilities towards them.

The PO is also responsible for conveying the product vision as seen by the investors to the entire Scrum team and ensures that the product is actually developed in accordance to the vision.

The Product Owner might need to take a back seat at times to allow the team to self-organize. This will require patience as well as faith. A good Product Owner will foster an efficient Scrum team - one that improves with each iteration and takes on bigger challenges.

The Product Owner is the single individual who is responsible for the success of the project. The Scrum Product Owner communicates his or her vision to the software development team, outlines work to be completed in the backlog, and prioritizes it based on business value.

Of course, he or she must also work closely with stakeholders (to ensure their interests are reflected in the product) and the software development team (to ensure the product is developed on time and within budget). As such, the Scrum Product Owner must be freely available to the development team to provide direction and answer questions.

However, this mix of authority and availability to the team makes it difficult for the Product Owner to resist the temptation to micro-manage. Because the Scrum method of agile software development values self-organization, it is the Product Owner's responsibility to respect the team's ability to complete its work based on its own plan.

This means that a Product Owner cannot add work mid-sprint. Even if requirements change or a chief competitor takes a product to market that renders plans irrelevant, the Product Owner must wait until the next sprint planning meeting to redirect a team's trajectory. (You can imagine how difficult it is to maintain a hands-off approach to management when deadlines draw near and customers make last-minute demands.)

Moreover, the Scrum Product Owner is responsible for constantly considering what activities will yield the highest business value. This means making difficult - even unpopular - decisions during the sprint planning meeting.

But, again, because the Product Owner is the single individual who takes the heat if the project fails, he or she must aggressively stake out what aspects of a product are critical, when they are built, and so on.

Just as the team has a responsibility to deliver the negotiated work to the Product Owner, the Product Owner is obliged to deliver the product to the customer, according to the customer's specifications.

Chapter 8

Scrum Impediments

In the Scrum method of agile development, a scrum impediment is defined as anything that stands in the way of a team's productivity. This can literally be anything, from a team member who isn't pulling his or her weight to an uncomfortably warm team room. But if it's keeping the team from working at optimal efficiency, it's an impediment.

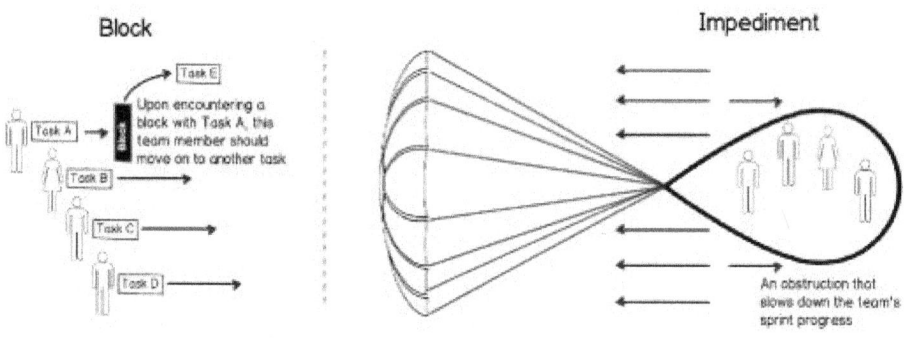

Luckily, Scrum dedicates an entire role to the resolution of these impediments: the ScrumMaster. The ScrumMaster works in a variety of capacities, such as helping the Product Owner prepare the backlog or radiating Scrum artifacts, but the primary responsibility of a ScrumMaster is to remove scrum impediments and facilitate a highly performing team.

To help the ScrumMaster achieve this, the team is responsible for communicating what barriers are impeding their progress. This occurs each day in the daily Scrum, when team members report on their accomplishments for the past 24 hours, goals for the next 24 hours, and what scrum impediments stand in their way. This systematized feedback loop ensures that a ScrumMaster always knows what is keeping the team from success and work to remove them.

Scrum Impediments can apply to an organization's adoption of the Scrum method of agile software development, as well. Just as a broken keyboard, for example, would hinder a team member from coding, an attitude resistant to change (a "culture clash") bars a smooth Scrum adoption.

In instances such as these, a company needs an organizational advocate to persuade management of the benefits of Scrum. In essence, that advocate is functioning as a ScrumMaster by eliminating barriers to productivity even before a single Scrum team has been created.

Of course, even an internal Scrum advocate does not ensure that a company will clearly see the potential of Scrum and migrate to agile practices. But, like the ScrumMaster who works closely with a team to remove impediments, an internal Scrum advocate can help enact positive change and contribute toward an organization's success with Scrum.

Scrum: Removing Sprint Planning Impediments

As described in other chapters, the scrum master may need to organize meetings to co-ordinate the stakeholder and product owner if this is not happening as necessary. This is not a must for the scrum master and only happens if lack of requirements is an impediment for the scrum team.

Prior to planning them, the product owner's decisions should be translated into user stories with acceptance criteria and prioritized into the backlog. At this point, the backlog may be complete, but in order for any of its stories to be ready for a sprint planning session, we need to ask the question, Does the team have everything it needs to complete this story?

There are often identifiable dependencies such as third-party feeds, specification documents or points of contact that need to be supplied in order for a team to do its job. The best way to know if a story is ready for planning is to be aware of what the team's roles are and do everything possible to keep them focused on their role.

E.g. a software developer should be spending as much time as possible developing software as opposed to contacting third-parties for specifications, a tester should be checking for quality instead of waiting for third-party software to come in. These are examples of impediments for the scrum master. A product owner will need to do as much research as possible to prevent these situations arising for the scrum master.

Sprint Pre-Planning

There are often situations where background discussion is necessary to keep the scrum time-boxes running smoothly. For example, the scrum master and product owner should work hard to make sure that the sprint planning meeting is not the place to find out that a user story is not ready for the team, or that acceptance criteria is too vague. Do not get me wrong, sometimes this is unavoidable, since nobody thinks like a team of experts. However, confusion should be avoided wherever possible.

For these reasons, I recommend that a product backlog grooming meeting is held each sprint and optionally before each sprint where necessary a preparation meeting take place. Here the scrum master (organizer and facilitator) product owner and tester gather to review the proposed sprint backlog.

The product owner presents the backlog, the scrum master usually has enough technical knowledge to know if stories are ready for the team, the tester knows if the acceptance criteria will meet entry-level requirements.

Chapter 9

The Scrum Checklist Rules

Understanding the fundamentals of scrum is a very simple thing to do. However putting it into practice in the world of deadlines, strong characters and the need for quick decisions can often make it a huge challenge to get the job done using the scrum rules. There are often situations where the rules are forgotten and put to one side, especially when they are most needed.

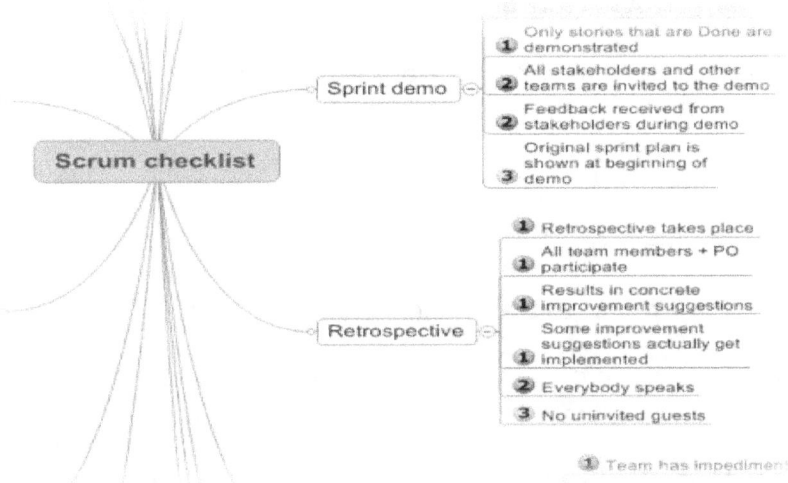

In my experience as a scrum master, team lead and software engineer I saw how easy it is for employees of a fast moving business to put the scrum rules to one side and destroy the very framework that would help make their daily lives easier.

Observing how easy it is to forget the fundamental elements of scrum, I have put together this simple checklist that anyone can use on a daily basis. It covers:

• Checklists for the fundamental tasks of every scrum role

• An overview and recap of each scrum meeting (time-box)

• Checklists for the preparation, carrying-out and goals of every scrum meeting

Using these checklists, you can be prepared and confident that you are carrying out the scrum practices on your daily job, boosting the productivity of your scrum team and increasing return on investment for the business. One section of the check list is below.

The SCRUM MASTER checklist

• update list of impediments from daily scrum, emails and other contact

• follow up on impediments above

• order any team equipment

• write sprint report to stake holders (once a sprint)

• chase up any information holding up sprint backlog (e.g. third party supplied artifacts)

• make sure burndown and task board are visible in team room

• arrange meetings and have chats to coach any new or needy team members, product owners or stakeholders

The PRODUCT OWNER checklist

• update backlog daily with any changes

• prioritize backlog daily based on business value

• meet stakeholders when needed to coordinate and capture requirements

• liaise with team to clarify requirements and make tradeoffs communicate release plan to stakeholders

The DEVELOPMENT TEAM checklist

• update task board with time remaining on tasks

• report any impediments to scrum master

• communicate with product owner before attempting and after completing a story

• achieve daily targets

• maintain team communication

• keep solutions simple

• focus on ship-ability (e.g. using practices such as pair programming, code review, continuous refactoring.

Chapter 10

Scrum Sprint

In the Scrum method of agile software development, work is confined to a regular, repeatable work cadence, known as a scrum sprint or iteration. In by-

the-book Scrum, a sprint lasts 30 days, but many teams prefer shorter work cycles, such as one-week, two-week, or three-week sprints.

How long each sprint actually is should be left to the discretion of a Scrum team, who must consider the advantages or disadvantages of a longer or shorter sprint for their specific development environment. The important thing is that a scrum sprint is a consistent, repeatable duration.

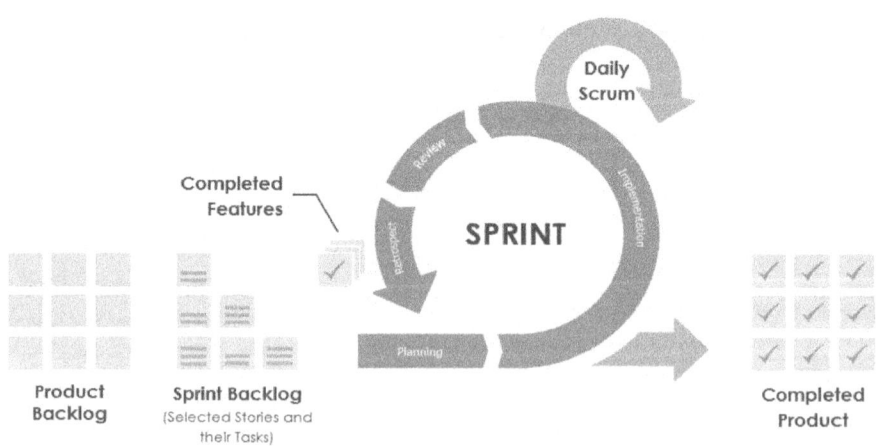

During each scrum sprint, a team works to create a shippable product - even in the first sprint. Of course, the shippable product the team develops in the first cycle of work wouldn't be ready to present to the customer.

Working within the limitations of such a short time, the team would only be able to build the most essential functionality. However, an emphasis on working code forces the Product Owner to prioritize a release's most essential features, helps developers focus on short-term goals, and shows customers tangible progress that they can respond to with more directed feedback.

Because it will require many sprints to satisfactorily complete the release, each iteration of work builds on the previous. As such, the Scrum method of agile software development is described as "iterative" and "incremental."

Each scrum sprint begins with the sprint planning meeting (I'll discuss the meetings of Scrum in later posts), in which the Product Owner and the team negotiate what stories in the product backlog will be moved into the sprint backlog.

The Product Owner is responsible for determining "what" the team will work on, while they retain the freedom to choose "how" to complete the work over the course of the sprint.

Once the team commits to the work for a sprint, the Product Owner must respect this commitment and refrain from adding work, changing course mid-sprint, or micromanaging in general.

Throughout the scrum sprint, teams check in through the daily Scrum meeting, also known as the daily standup. This time-boxed meeting gives teams an opportunity to update project status, discuss solutions to impediments, and radiate progress to the Product Owner (who may or may not attend this meeting, but, when attending, may only observe or answer the team's questions).

The scrum sprint concludes with the sprint review meeting, in which the team presents its work to the Product Owner. During this meeting, the Product Owner must determine whether the team's work has or has not met each story's acceptance criteria.

If a release does not satisfy each criterion, it is rejected as incomplete and, typically, added to the sprint backlog for the next sprint. If it satisfies the established criteria, then the team receives the full number of points associated with the story and it is designated "done."

Because some sprints are tremendous successes and others like treading water, a team meets each sprint to discuss what worked, what didn't, and how processes could be improved. This meeting is called the sprint retrospective meeting.

Scrum Sprint Zero

When an organization is ready to run its first project using Scrum, it's often unclear about how to get started. The rules are very detailed about processes once the first sprint has begun, but how does a team prepare for that?

For many Scrum authorities, the answer is a sprint zero - or a preliminary sprint which is exclusively dedicated to getting ready for the first sprint. But what this iteration includes, how long it lasts, and even what it's called varies depending on who you talk to.

Personally, I think this iteration should focus on setting up the team's physical environment, i.e. setting up computers, creating a team room, optimizing work stations, and so on. Others, however, argue that sprint zero is an opportunity to prepare the team for its first planning meeting.

In addition to creating a conducive work environment, that sprint entails adding a few substantial items to the backlog and writing a piece of real, functioning code - no matter how basic. After all, if the first activity of the first sprint is the sprint planning meeting, a Product Owner will want to have something in the backlog to start with.

Given that requirements gathering can often lead to analysis paralysis, I feel that this time should be as short as possible - just long enough to accomplish the few preparatory goals listed above.

Others, however, firmly believe that iteration zero should be the duration of a regular sprint to help teams establish a rhythm. Unsurprisingly, those who argue for a sprint zero reflecting the established time and culture cadence also assert that sprint zero could just as easily be called sprint one.

Their primary reason for this stance is that the basic goals of sprint zero - which address design, infrastructure, process improvement, implementation, test, and validation - are goals of every sprint.

For Scrum practitioners in this camp, getting started may require more administrative work, but the principles of removing impediments and writing functional code remain intact.

The sprint zero concept is contentious among Scrum practitioners. Though they might not all agree on whether it's necessary, what it should be called, or how long it should last, the good news is that sprint zero preserves the principles and processes of the sprints to follow.

The Sprint Planning Meeting

Scrum consists of Sprints or iterations which are time boxed events. This means that the Sprint starts and ends at a fixed time, irrespective of whether its goals are met. Sprint duration may range from one week to four weeks. One week may be too little time to produce something tangible or potentially shippable. A team may experiment with various durations until it realizes which one is the best for them.

Sprint Goal

The goal of the Sprint in Scrum is to produce a potentially shippable product or functionality. This could be in the form of one or many features of the product that is being built. 'Potentially shippable 'means that all the aspects of the feature are built - it is designed per requirements, coded, tested and approved. Although there may not be an actual release at the end of every Sprint, the work done is release ready.

Duration

The Sprint Planning Meeting is limited to 8 hours for a 4 week Sprint. The meeting is shorter for shorter Sprints - for example, a two week Sprint would have a four hour planning meeting.

Structure of the Sprint Planning Meeting

The Sprint Planning Meeting can be broadly split into two parts. The first part deals with 'what' will be done in that Sprint. The other part deals with 'how' the 'what' will be achieved.

The presence of the Product Owner is imperative for the first half. This is when the Product Owner orders the Product Backlog and explains what the topmost priority for the business is.

The team uses this input to decide how much it can take on in that particular Sprint. The team may choose one or many items off the Product Backlog depending on the size of the items and the time needed to build them. The team uses experience and historic data to decide how much they can handle. Scrum encourages teams to take responsibility and decide their capacity themselves.

The second part of the Sprint Planning Meeting addresses 'how' the team will actually handle the work it has taken on. The Product Owner can leave the room at this time, but should be available to answer any questions the team has.

The team is allowed to plan how they will handle the work, and who will do what task. The idea here is that each person does what they are best at, but is available and willing to pitch in for any other tasks as needed.

Chapter 11

Scrum User Stories, Retrospective And Epic

Scrum User Stories

○ Story ID:	Story Title:	
User Story:		**Importance:**
As a: <role> I want: <some goal> So that: <some reason>		
		Estimate:
Acceptance Criteria		**Type:**
And I know I am done when:		☐ Search ☐ Workflow ☐ Manage Data ☐ Payment ☐ Report/ View

In the Scrum method of agile software development, user stories are how work is expressed in the backlog. How a team decides to write its user stories is a matter of preference, but the user story must always be written from the perspective of the end user.

That is, team members are encouraged to conceive of their work from the standpoint of the consumer who will use it (hence "user" story).

A team might articulate a story as a noun or, more specifically, a feature to be built into a product, such as "text message" on a cell phone project or "speedometer" for an automobile manufacturer. Or the story could be stated in a sentence or phrase, such as "debug GPS tracking system."

Many Scrum teams have adopted Mike Cohn's user story template, in which a single sentence identifies who the end user is, what the end user wants, and why. This model of a user story is typically written like this: "As a [end user role], I want [the desire] so that [the rationale].

By way of illustration without placeholders, consider how a user story for a developer working on a calculator application for a PC might express the work.

First, he would need to know who he is coding the application for: a PC user. Secondly, he would want to determine what the PC user would want to use the application for: to have a convenient prepackaged calculator application.

Finally, he would want to state why it's important that the PC user have this application. This is perhaps the least clearly defined piece of information, but one can assume that the developer might state the rationale would be to add, subtract, multiply, and divide-or to simply add value to the product.

Thus the final user story might read something like this: "As a PC user, I want a calculator with basic functionality on my PC so that I can conveniently perform basic mathematic operations and enhance my overall experience."

User stories are a way to document requirements from the perspective of the end user. Although stories can be written in a number of ways, Mike Cohn's model is of particular value for Scrum development teams because it provides the most information about the story, including for whom it is being built and why. By orienting the story to reflect the desires of the end user, user stories help developers remain focused on what the customer wants.

SPRINT RETROSPECTIVE OBJECTIVES

01 What worked or went well?

02 What caused problems, failed to work properly, or did not go well?

03 What can be done differently in the next sprint to improve the process and overcome the problems occurring previously?

When the sprint ends in Scrum, it's time for the team to present its work to the Product Owner for approval. This process is known as the sprint review meeting. In this meeting, the Product Owner goes through the stories assigned for the sprint and asks the team to present the work.

The Product Owner checks the work to make sure it has addressed all the acceptance criteria outlined in the product backlog item. (In some cases, a team may have met all the criteria, but the end product still isn't what the Product Owner wants.

In such a case, the team would be awarded points for creating a product that satisfied the acceptance criteria, but the Product Owner would likely re-write the story for the team to tackle in the next sprint.) Even if 99 percent of a story is completed by a team, the Product Owner must reject it as incomplete.

Many teams find that the finishing touches on a product are often the most labor-intensive and time-consuming, so awarding partial credit for unfinished work can contribute to a misleading velocity. This is the "inspect" phase of Scrum's inspect-and-adapt approach to software development.

Following the sprint review meeting the team holds a scrum retrospective meeting with the ScrumMaster. At this time, the team discusses three things: what went well, what didn't go well, and what improvements could be made in the next sprint. Because the Product Owner does not attend this meeting, it's an opportunity to speak candidly about successes and failures.

This is an especially important opportunity for the team to focus on its overall performance and identify strategies to improve its processes. Similarly, it's a valuable chance for the ScrumMaster, who can observe common impediments affecting the team and work to resolve them. This meeting, which is usually time-boxed at three hours, represents the "adapt" phase of the inspect-and-adapt approach.

In short, the Scrum method of agile software development uses the sprint review and scrum retrospective meetings to reinforce Scrum's emphasis on transparency and communication. By formalizing communication with these meetings, Scrum ensures that every team member is informed and connected.

Scrum Epics

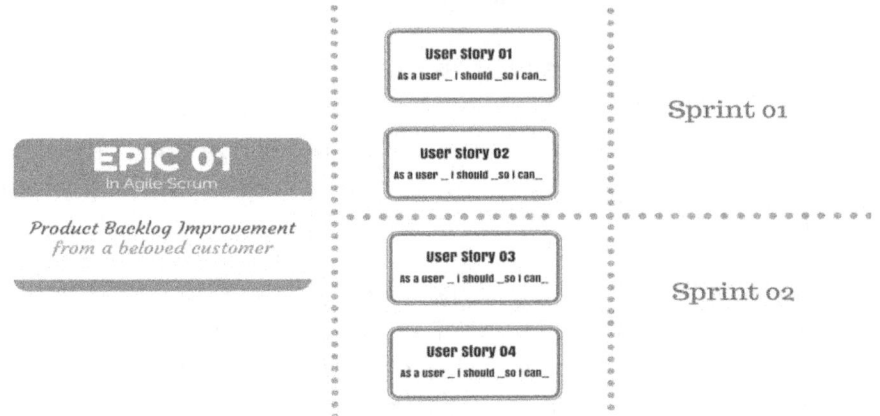

In the Scrum method of agile software development, each user story is assigned a corresponding effort estimate by the team that will complete the work. But what happens when a team can't settle on an appropriate estimate? What if a story includes too many variables to really know how big it is? Or what if its requirements are known, but its effort is off the charts?

Such stories are called "epics." While a typical story is expected to be completed in four to sixteen hours, an epic usually refers to a story that would require twelve - or many more - hours to complete.

Most Scrum experts recommend that, if a story's tasks will require 12 or more hours, it should be broken down - or decomposed - into its constituent stories. These decomposed stories will be smaller, more narrowly defined. In essence, this practice of decomposing epics simply helps a development team translate its work into manageable chunks of work.

But what's the danger of estimating an epic? A best guess can't hurt, right? Actually, estimating epics is potentially harmful because it deludes a Product Owner into the belief that the requirements, tasks, and effort of the epic are known. Let me explain. When a team estimates an epic, that estimation is seldom limited to a kind of best-guess reference for the team.

More commonly, that estimate is used as the basis for forecasting, which, in turn, forms the basis of a budget. At that stage, that best guess has suddenly become an inflexible projection that commits a team to perform an unknown amount of work within a fixed budget.

This approach is like going to the grocery store with a set amount of money to spend, but no list of what to buy. Clearly, someone in that scenario would have a lot of questions. What dish am I preparing? What ingredients does it include?

And, if I can't budget for all of those ingredients, which ones are most essential? Basically, this hypothetical shopper has no idea how to accomplish the task at hand. The same goes for the Product Owner - who commits to an estimate of a story when there is little information surrounding the project's requirements.

Chapter 12

Scrum Teams

For Scrum software development, an ideal team consists of seven members, plus or minus two. Usually, Scrum teams are made of cross-functional members, who include a mix of software engineers, architects, programmers, analysts, QA experts, testers, UI designers, and so on. In Scrum, it is recommended that the team is located in a single room (the team room).

Although the Scrum team is responsible for the completion of the work agreed upon in the Sprint Planning Meeting, the team has the ability to limit the amount of work it takes on. Granted, the Product Owner will expect the team to take on as many story points of work as can be realistically completed.

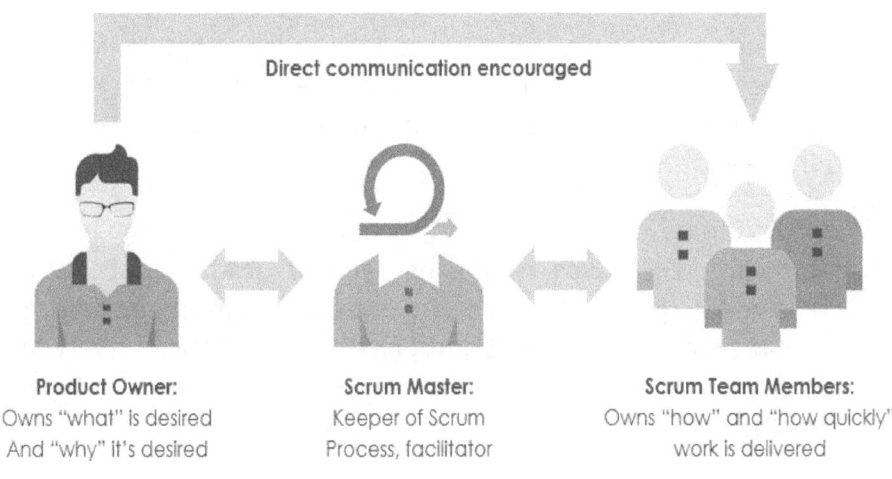

Direct communication encouraged

Product Owner:
Owns "what" is desired
And "why" it's desired

Scrum Master:
Keeper of Scrum
Process, facilitator

Scrum Team Members:
Owns "how" and "how quickly"
work is delivered

In this case, the Scrum team would point to its established velocity for previous sprints to negotiate how many story points constitute a realistic workload.) This process of negotiation is valuable for two reasons.

Firstly, it protects the team from being overwhelmed with an unreasonable sprint backlog. Secondly, it manages the expectations of the Product Owner, who, in turn, can do the same for customers.

Similarly, the team has the autonomy to determine how and when to complete its work. Provided that the team finishes its work on time and within budget, how that work is completed is entirely up to the discretion of the team. In theory, the team could spend the first half of its sprint at the beach, as long as the work meets the corresponding acceptance criteria.

Of course, a Scrum team typically needs the entire sprint to complete its work. In fact, it's common for Scrum teams to discover within the first few days of a sprint, when the team begins to wrap its heads around the work to be completed, that they have even more work to do than they originally thought. Moreover, the Scrum method of agile software development does not award partial credit.

Even if a project is 99 percent "done," it's still incomplete if it does not meet all the established acceptance criteria. After all, a project's finishing touches are often the most time-consuming and labor-intensive.

Using Scrum to manage agile software development is the leading strategy to help teams reduce risk and associated costs, while increasing the quality of a team's releases. Through an emphasis on communication and collaboration, Scrum brings everyone together--from developers to stakeholders--to build a better product.

Why Scrum Teams Should Be Small

One of the ways Scrum helps unite team members is through a mandate that teams remain small. Most Scrum literature recommends that teams be made up of seven cross-functional members (give or take two).

Certainly, limiting the number of "communication channels" allows teams to engage in high-impact collaboration without too much of a margin to leave anyone in the dark. In fact, there's a relatively straightforward equation to illustrate how, as team members are added and channels of communication increase, maintaining communication with the entire team becomes a considerable challenge.

The formula, in which "S" equals the number of communication channels and N stands for the number of team members, can be represented as: $S=(N(N-1))/2$

Interestingly, as team members are added, the value of "S" (i.e. the number of communication channels) rises dramatically. That is, if a team of six added two more developers to its team, the size of the group would increase to eight, but the total number of communication channels would balloon from 15 to 28. Suddenly the effort associated with communicating to every other team member has nearly doubled.

Although Scrum teams are recommended to be small, the framework guards against "group think," i.e. a passive herd mentality, by asking that teams be composed cross-functionally. In other words, Scrum teams should be created to represent a range of job functions without much overlap.

Where traditional, sequential development-better known as 'waterfall'-grouped teams by function (testing, QA, etc.), Scrum prefers that all "phases" of development be present in the single cross-functional team.

As such, a single Scrum team would likely include a mix of software engineers, architects, programmers, analysts, QA experts, testers, UI designers, and so on.

When individuals with different skill sets, areas of expertise, and development experience come together for the kind of collaboration that Scrum enables, it ensures that multiple perspectives are considered. In fact, when individuals with such diverse backgrounds brainstorm on a problem, they may hit on a new solution as a group that they couldn't have reached independently.

On the flip side, imagine a team of 20 trying to work together to resolve a particularly difficult problem. Because of the sheer number of people, a leader-or a handful of them-would likely emerge and, as a result, some team members might passively follow along.

Or something worse might happen: The size of the group might keep it from making a fully considered decision-or any decision at all.

How To Be a More Productive Scrum Team

1. Know The Scrum Guide Inside Out

This may seem almost obvious, but you would be surprised at the number of people that are employed as scrum masters but really do not have a rock solid knowledge on the simple fundamentals of scrum. Unfortunately, many people today are project managers who get the "jist" of scrum or know a few practices.

With that said, my first tip is to simply read and understand the scrum rules, based not only on experience and word of mouth, but on Ken Schwaber and Jeff Sutherland's official scrum guide.

I have found that most people learned scrum based on their experiences in companies, what they have read in books and what they have been told by others. This guide is the final word from the people who created the framework.

2. Stick To The Rules (Come What May)

This tip is very closely related to starting with the scrum rules, but subtly different. Whereas that rule was about starting on the correct foundation, this rule is all about sticking to that foundation throughout thick and thin. It may seem as if simple rules are easy to stick to, but any experienced scrum practitioner will tell you that "simple to understand" does not necessarily equal "easy to put into practice".

3. Trust The Scrum Framework (and Learn how to Leverage It)

Again, moving slightly on from the issue of sticking to the rules, my next tip is one of the most helpful ones in terms of achieving productivity in the simplest way possible. The beauty of this is that it arms us with the minimum set of tools we need to keep a project running smoothly.

Communication is managed through a 15 minute daily meeting, sprint review (demo) and retrospective. New features, risks, absenteeism and bugs are managed through a backlog, sprints and sprint planning every one to four weeks. Therefore, the framework is equipped to deal with any change on a daily basis and then review after each sprint.

4. Complement with the Agile Toolkit

Although there is a process and method involved in carrying out the framework, it is clearly described as a framework. The practices and rules are not the end of the story, just the beginning. To make a project potentially shippable, complement with practices such as: Test Driven Development, Pair Programming, Automated Testing and Continuous Build.

5. Trust the Team and learn how to leverage them

One major difference between scrum and many of its predecessors is the emphasis on the team as opposed to the other roles. Scrum empowers teams to organize themselves, make decisions and solve problems.

6. Respect motivates teams

Getting the most out of any project usually means getting the best out of the team involved. In my experience, I have discovered that teams will rarely work hard for people they do not respect. This can apply equally to anyone who interfaces with the project team.

7. Common Sense is the Golden Rule

The one rule that trumps all the other rules is the rule of common sense. Don't get me wrong. I am a strong believer that rules are NOT made to be broken. However there are specific times when specific practices do not make sense. In my experience I have never been forced to abandon any scrum rule or practice in the name of common sense. I think the beauty of the framework is that in general, it IS common sense.

Chapter 13

Scrum Burndown Charts

What is a burn down chart?

A burn down chart is an important tool in scrum. It provides a visual representation about the progress achieved in a sprint while it is underway. They are very common and extensively used by scrum masters while scrum is being implemented in a project. The quantity, or the amount of work remaining, in the form of pending tasks, is typically exhibited in a burn down chart.

The chart is simple and easy to understand, even by people who are not familiar with scrum methodology. Burn down charts are very useful for estimation purposes, and are essential for determining the sprint velocity - the rate at which work in the form of user stories is being completed by the development team - and planning the sprint release.

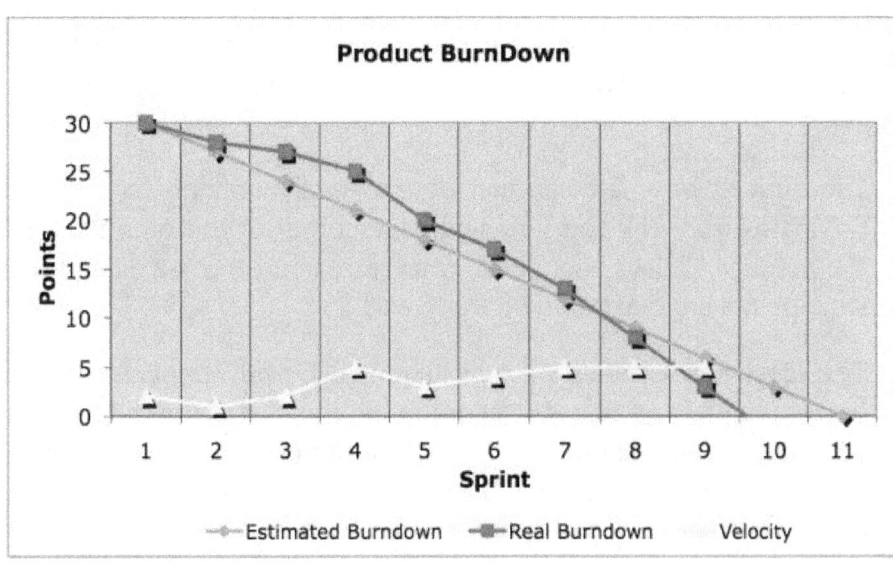

Plotting the burn down chart

A burn down chart can be plotted by including the work remaining in the form of story points along the vertical Y-axis and the working days along the horizontal X-axis.

The pending work is typically represented in story points - a unit of measurement to calculate the importance and priority of user stories in the sprint backlog - instead of user stories.

The reason is user stories are broken down into tasks during the second half of the sprint planning meeting by the development team. It becomes difficult to read and understand the chart if tasks are represented along the Y-axis.

User stories are descriptive in nature, and do not have a number or a value associated with them, so it becomes difficult to estimate them. Therefore, the story points, which are numeric values associated with each user story, are used for plotting purposes.

On the first day of the sprint, the total number of days completed in the sprint is zero while the pending work constitutes the entire sprint backlog. Conversely, when the entire sprint is processed, the number of days is equivalent to the days the sprint has actually lasted - generally two weeks - and the pending work should be zero.

The burn down chart can include an "ideal" working line, which originates from the top left-hand-side corner of the graph where the number of days is equivalent to zero along the X-axis and the story points are maximum on the Y-axis.

The ideal line extends or runs diagonally, and connects to the bottom right-hand-side of the graph, on the X-axis where the days are maximum i.e. equal to the total number of days the sprint lasts. The story points are zero on the Y-axis. The ideal line reflects the desired level of work and sprint completion status.

Starting from day zero, when the story points are maximum, as the sprint progresses, the days increase along the X-axis while the story points start decreasing along the Y-axis.

On day one, when some of the user stories are completed, a point is interpolated on the graph which correlated to the first day of the sprint on the X-axis and a value equal to the maximum story points in the sprint minus the value of story points completed on that day.

For example, if 25 story points are included in the sprint, and on day one of the sprint if work equal to 5 story points is completed, the total pending work remaining in the sprint is equivalent to 25 - 5 = 20 points. The coordinates of the point would be (0, 20) on the graph.

Similarly, on the second day of the sprint, if work equal to 1 story point is completed, the total work remaining is equivalent to 20 - 1 = 19 story points. The coordinates for the second day would be (1, 19) on the graph. Many scrum masters prefer the dates to be displayed along the X-axis in lieu of days to make the chart more readable.

Reading the chart

Many burn down charts actually have the "ideal" line plotted on them - for reference and estimation purposes. It is a good visual indication whether the particular sprint is proceeding as per schedule, or whether the development work is carried out behind schedule.

The line represents the ideal "burn down" required for attaining the sprint goal or the ideal position to be in at the end of sprinting day. The actual work carried out is plotted on the graph with the help of coordinate points. All the points plotted on the graph are connected with a line, which passes through them.

If the actual line extends above the ideal line, it indicates that the sprint is proceeding behind schedule, and the required number of tasks is not being completed as per the sprint planning.

This basically indicates two things - one, the team has to put in more efforts to compensate for the pending work which should be completed the next working day, and two - the team is required to introspect and find out why the tasks were not completed on time. It is important to self-correct and ensure the same mistakes are not repeated since scrum advocates self-learning and self-correction processes.

Chapter 14

Estimating Ideas From Scrum

Scrum has some interesting ideas to overcome the perennial challenge of accurate estimating. In this chapter I'd like to have a look at a collection of those approaches: story points, burn-down velocities and planning poker. Scrum is generally used for software development projects, but the ideas in this chapter could be applied to any type of work.

Key ideas of User Stories

- They **highlight negotiation** to happen between the customer and the team.

- User stories help deferring details till later
- They talk problems not solutions
- They fit nicely as your Product Backlog items

Step 1 - Collect Together User Stories

In Scrum each project is broken down into a collection of user stories. These are descriptions of a single piece of functionality that the delivered software must perform.

They are really requirements, requirements sound mandatory, and much of what users initially ask for are "nice to haves." Each user story describes a journey through the software. For example, a story might say, "Log on using your user name and password and be taken to the home screen."

The software team will work with their clients to decide on which user stories will be delivered during the next sprint of work. Sprints generally last around 20 days. To do this the development team need to estimate the work involved with each user story. This is where the ideas of user points and planning poker are useful.

Step 2 - Estimate Each User Story In Terms of Story Points

One estimating pitfall is confusing effort (the number of hours something takes to do) with duration (over what period of calendar time something takes to do.)

For example, a developer might say a user story will take eight hours to complete and the team will assume he can do it in one day. However when he starts work he finds he has other time commitments, and can only work on the story for an hour a day. Eight days later he finishes the task.

Durations are difficult to estimate; we all have good days and bad days and some days have more interruptions than others. Scrum's answer to this is to move the team entirely away from estimating times and instead estimate each user story in terms of story points. Story points are an abstract measure of size.

The best way of using story points is to start off with the first user story and give it a certain size, for example ten story points. Then, for the next story, ask the question, how big is this compared to the first one? If it is half the size it is assigned five story points. This relative comparison helps to anchor a size in the estimator's mind.

Step 3 - Playing Planning Poker

Planning poker is a good way of estimating story points. Each team member is given a set of "poker" playing cards. Each card has a number on it, representing a story point estimate.

Typically each team member has about 20 cards. Rather than use cards of one to twenty, the fibonacci series is often used (1,2,3,5,8,13,21,34 and so on). The variation in the gaps between the fibonacci numbers represents the inherent uncertainty with estimating.

The "poker" game then starts. A user story is presented to the team, then each team member selects a card representing their estimate and places if face down on the table.

All the cards are turned over simultaneously. This is important, as otherwise one person's estimate might sway another's. A discussion follows where developers justify their estimate. This process is repeated several times.

Step 4 - Using Velocity to Convert Story Points To Duration

Story points are abstract, so now the team convert them to duration to see how much time it will take to develop a collection of user stories of a certain user point size. This is where the Scrum concept of velocity comes in. Velocity is a measure of how much work a team can do in a typical day. In other words

Velocity = Story points/Duration

So if a user story is 30 story points big and the team's typical velocity is three story points per day, the user story should take 10 calendar days to complete. The next question of course is what is the velocity of your team?

Well the best way of estimating this is by doing a few sprints and seeing how much work the team does on an average day. If it is the first sprint, the team will have to come together and make a reasonable estimate of their likely velocity (maybe by using planning poker again).

Burndown charts are a useful tool to help a team monitor its work and calculate their velocity. They show, on a day-by-day basis, how many user points remain to be done. Every day the team is asked to recalculate how many story points remain and this figure is plotted on the graph.

This figure hopefully goes down, although sometimes as the team gets into a piece of work, they will realize that their initial estimates were too low. The slope of the burndown chart is the velocity of the team.

Estimating is always difficult, no-one has a crystal ball to be able to see into the future, but the Scrum ideas of user points and planning poker give an approach which helps for collaborative discussion and thought which should give more accurate predictions.

Monitoring a team's velocity using burndown charts help to give useful historical information for future estimating and also transparency of where the team are in the development process at any particular time.

Chapter 15

How Do We Scale Scrum?

The scrum framework brings structure and order to a project in a chaotic, fast-paced environment. It delivers a shippable increment of the product after each sprint and allows a business to increase return on investment through prioritization.

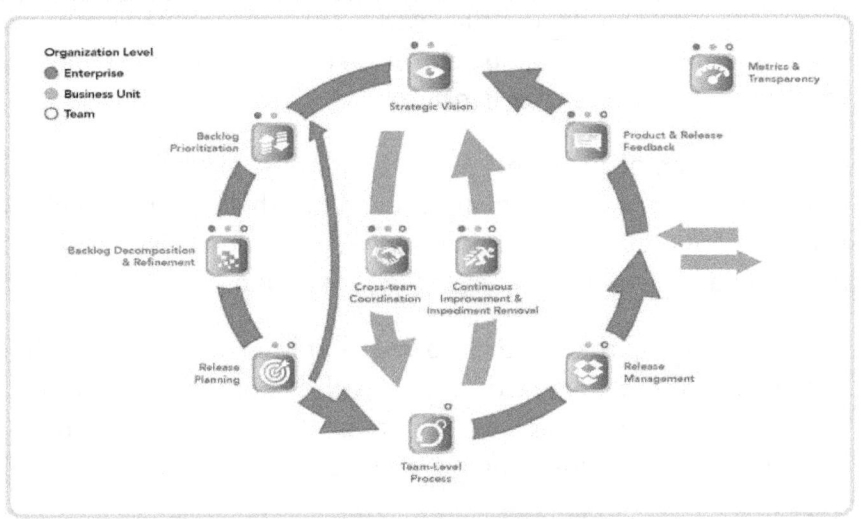

As long as the rules are carried out as its creators intended the results are phenomenal and business value is realized. However what happens when the business requires greater output, many related projects to be synchronized to a deadline or a co-ordinated technical solution? This is where the technique comes into its own.

The Scrum of scrums is a method of co-coordinating teams and is used to grow and synchronize the scrum framework within a company to huge scale. As a scrum master I have used this technique to great effect in order to keep complex inter-related projects in sync.

1. The Challenge - Scaling

The challenge in scaling across an organization lies within the rule that a team should typically have between five and nine members. While this is a guideline and there is no substitute for common sense, teams should definitely be "lean, mean productive machines".

The challenge gets interesting when the business stakeholders wake up one morning and say "I want to deliver quicker, let's put another thirty people on the project". Or if they say "we need this delivered in three months and there are three other dependent teams you need to deliver this with." Breaking the news that you want to limit the team to nine members would seem to limit the ability of the business to deliver.

This technique helps in these very situations, but before I explain how it works it is important to understand that it relies on all the original rules of scrum being carried out correctly, especially product backlog management and prioritization.

For this reason, the product owner's role is key to the whole process and this should be discussed with the product owner(s) and stakeholders involved before embarking on a this mission in your organization. Continue reading and you will see why this is so important.

2. What is Scrum of Scrums?

This is a meeting held to co-ordinate a set of inter-related scrum teams. The power and ability to scale is in the fact that one representative from each related team attends the meeting. By doing this an organization can co-ordinate hundreds of people on different teams.

From each team, a representative has been picked to attend the meeting. The representatives share knowledge.

Once the number of members in the scrum of scrums becomes too large a representative from that meeting can join another meeting and the process can continue.

In this meeting, the host asks four questions (in the same vein as the daily scrum meeting). The questions are:

1. What have you accomplished since the last meeting

2. What do you aim to accomplish before the next meeting

3. Are there any impediments/blockers in your way

4. Are you about to do anything that could create a blocker/impediment to the project

The first three questions aim to highlight progress, draw attention to targets and surface any issues that need to be addressed to keep the project on track. The last question stems from the fact that related projects can often unknowingly create problems for each other. For example, in the technology world, one team may deploy code that means vastly more testing for another team.

The meetings can be scheduled to be as frequent needed and are usually anywhere from daily to bi-weekly. It purely depends on the needs of the programme.

Chapter 16

Relevance Of Embracing Scrum To Rescue A Project

The three reasons below justify why a project should be moved to Scrum:

Incremental, uninterrupted delivery at the conclusion of the project

After the completion of overall planning, analysis and designing of a project does only the delivery happen with a Waterfall model. However, at the culmination of every 2 weeks does the delivery happen in minor portions which enables all stakeholders and the project board(s) concerned in a Scrum project to realize the achievements.

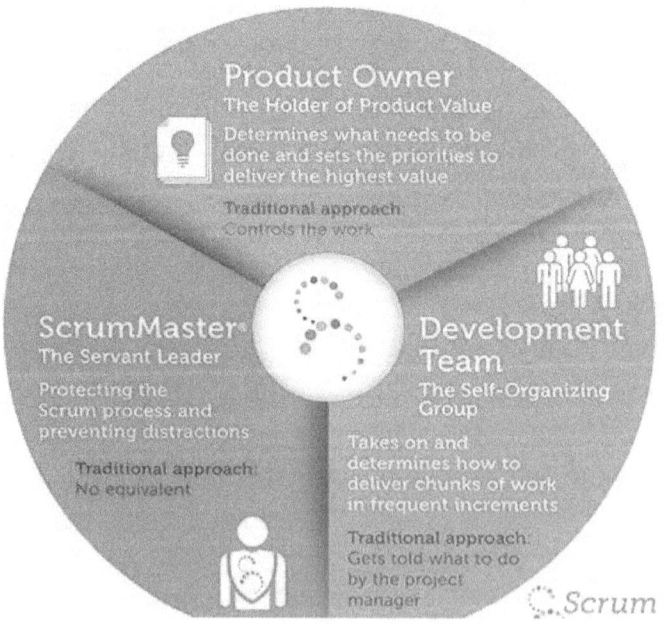

Heightened clearness and transparency

Scrum involves having a clear vision as to the list related with product delivery as well as the delivery order, after which execution of work, forthright commitment declaration towards that list before the end of that 2 week duration must be carried out. A board is required to envision the work they are focused on whereby valuable lessons are imbibed from mistakes.

Improved control

A strong discipline is required of the team members executing a Scrum project as Product Owners have the liberty to alter their perception (acceptance benchmarks which the team needs to adhere to) about the delivery order of products for every 2 weeks interval at the commencement of every single sprint.

Accepting the necessary role and importance of a Scrum Master

Lack of discipline in adhering to the standards laid down by Product Owners will always result in the team not achieving the benefits of Scrum for which an experienced Scrum Master is required of who can help the team in transitioning the project towards Scrum, educating the team about Scrum rules, shaping the team towards better usage of Scrum, making stakeholders understand the value of their support towards the project and monitoring the team's work, checking to ensure team members do not do a U-turn towards past ineffective habits.

Conducting a Scrum training involving all necessary stakeholders

All stakeholders including the team should be made aware of the processes, roles, control mechanisms and basic rules of Scrum so that when everyone starts working on a Scrum project, they can coordinate and work using a common language (which can happen by working right through real time projects using Scrum). It can be done through relevant documentations available, case studies, anecdotes etc.

Transitioning to a Scrum-oriented governance standard related with the daily project execution

Integration of PRINCE2 with Scrum can do wonders for a project as role clarification and realization of improved mitigation of risk and tolerances of projects can be achieved much more in a simplified manner.

However, to satisfy Project Boards regarding reports, the team(s) can make use of statistics in terms of the level of commitment by the team and the delivery with the expected set estimates etc. in the line of Project controls set by PRINCE2.

Allocating physical space for the Team(s) involved with Scrum Project

It's vital to get authorization (if it was not there initially) for making use of some amount of physical space for the team as the team will need to - make use of white boards, put up sticky notes regarding WIP or work-in-progress communication.

Creating the Product Backlog

The product backlog helps in comparing the requirements of stakeholders with the outcomes of the project through delving in to the list of products, and obtaining feedback from users regarding their expectations of what and when regarding delivery will play a significant role in communication transparency.

Chapter 17

Create An Effective Product Vision To Succeed With Scrum

Even under normal circumstances, it is exceedingly important for a team or business organization to have vision. It is this mission that guides strategy, tactics and everyday tasks. Having an effective visualization is even more important when one is talking about the scrum methodology.

Many a times, a scrum project fails simply because the team members were not clear about the overall goal. It is therefore critical to come up with an effective product-vision to succeed with a scrum project. Here is how you can create such a product-vision.

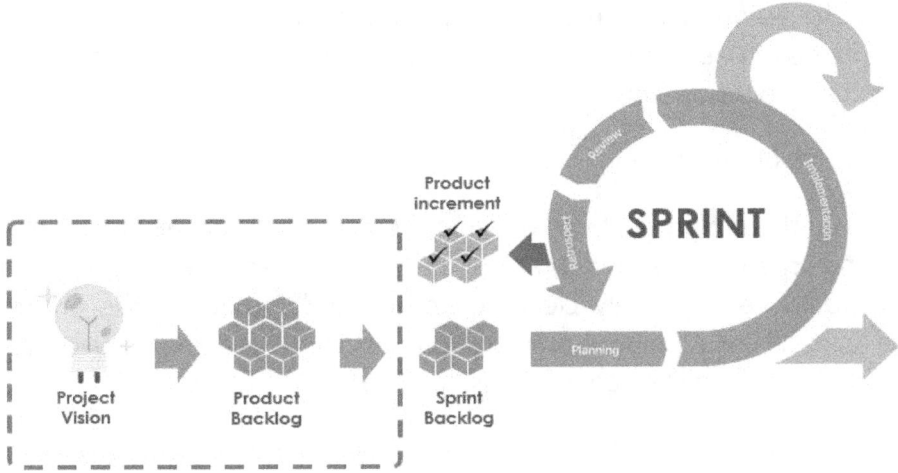

Making It Customer Centric

An important hallmark of an effective product vision is the fact that it is completely customer or user centric. The team has to address questions such as:

• Where is the target user or customer?

• How will the purchase decision be made?

• Who will actually buy the product?

• Who are its nearest competitors?

• What makes the product unique?

• What emotional connect will the customer have with the product?

The Vision Is Everything

When it comes to creating a product-vision, everybody within the scrum ecosystem needs to know and internalize the fact that it is the vision that is paramount and overrides every other aspect. This "supremacy" of the vision is equally applicable to all the team members, the scrum Master, customers, top management and product owner and so on.

If the vision has been created by involving all the stakeholders of the scrum ecosystem, then everybody will have a buy in as far as this vision is concerned.

Clarity of Vision

Even though product visualization is created by bringing in tangible and intangible product attributes or qualities, the vision itself should be extremely clear and easily understood by the entire team. Having a blurry or ambiguous vision will not help in creating or succeeding in scrum projects.

Even though it is a result of a lot of work and brainstorming, once it has been conceptualized and stated, it should be capable of being described in just a few lines. Brevity is certainly the soul of successful product vision.

Making It All Tangible

Typically, while creating a vision, there are a lot of attributes and intangible values that are attached to a product. This may take a long time to crystallize. It will need quite a bit of homework to be done as well. Once the product concept has been developed, then it is extremely important to make it a tangible entity rather than leaving it at the concept stage.

Chapter 18

Steps To A Scrum Transformation

Transitioning to scrum is no easy task, no matter the size of the organization. The larger the organization the more difficult it will be. I've seen far too many companies spending exorbitant amounts in transforming to agile, yet fail in its attempts. I found that it is the direction or lack of that plays a major factor. Here are three steps you need to take to get you started in the right direction.

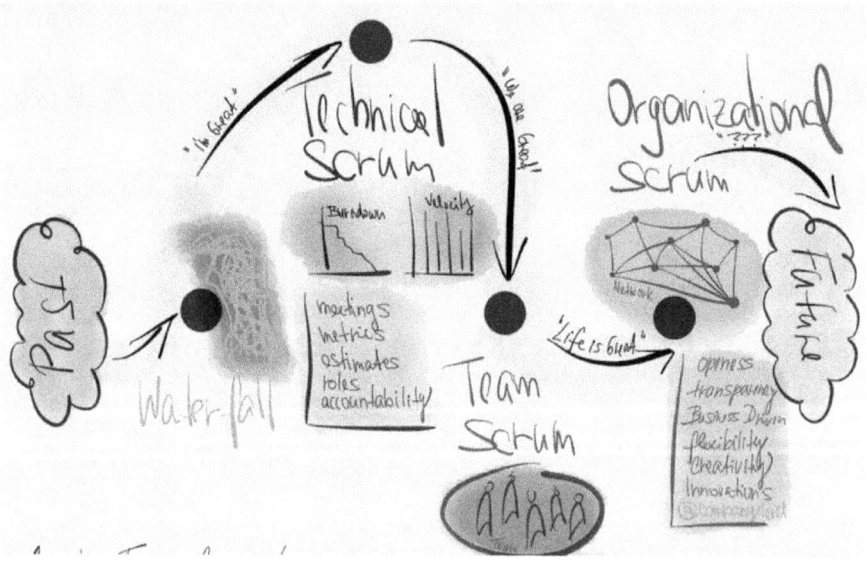

Step 1:

I have found the best way to transition is to start with a goal and understanding of why you are moving in this direction. Transitioning to agile is trendy, but not a good reason to take your organization through it. So what is your reason? Do you want to align business and IT? Or do you want to increase your speed to market? Do you want to increase team performance? Understand why and communicate it.

Step 2:

Outline your goals. Do your goals agree with the reason you choose to transition? If they don't, go back and review. Establishing the goals will help you focus.

Step 3:

Consider the type of transition. Is this an enterprise transformation to Agile or a departmental one? If it is a departmental approach, make sure you reach out to all the departments that your team will interact to get their work done.

Make an agreement with these other line managers upfront that will cover approvals that may be required, change in process that may need to be made. Remember the goal is to remove as many obstacles early on out of the teams way as possible.

Step 4:

Understand your organizations corporate culture. Be prepare for the obstacles ahead. Is there something you can do to help change the culture to be more conducive to Agile thinking? If not, plan on how your team will be protected.

Keep in mind Scrum is all about self-organized teams. These teams solve problems and make decisions on the spot. If your corporate culture is not in alignment with this and other scrum values, your team will be hitting brick in no time.

Step 5:

Choose the right project! Never ever start with a project that is a high risk project. This would be disastrous. Start with a project that is low risk and mid-sized. There is enough complexity to the transition, you don't need to add to it by selecting the wrong project.

Step 6:

Using the goals from step 2 create an assessment. Baseline where you are today. This will help you monitor and drive the progress of the transition.

Chapter 19

Minimizing Risks Through Scrum

Being an Agile, iterative process, the Scrum framework inherently minimizes risk. The following Scrum practices facilitate the effective management of risk:

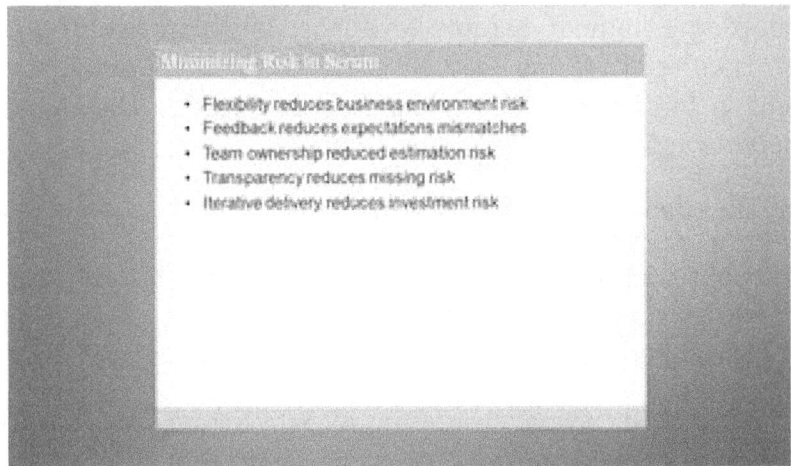

1. Flexibility reduces business-environment-related risk

Risk is largely minimized in Scrum due to the flexibility in adding or modifying requirements at any time in the project lifecycle. This enables the organization to respond to threats or opportunities from the business environment and unforeseen requirements whenever they arise, with usually low cost of managing such risks.

2. Regular feedback reduces expectations-related risk

Being iterative, the Scrum framework gives ample opportunities to obtain feedback and set expectations throughout the project lifecycle. This ensures that the project stakeholders, as well as the team, are not caught off guard by miscommunicated requirements.

3. Team ownership reduces estimation risk

The Scrum Team estimates and takes ownership of the Sprint Backlog Items, which leads to more accurate estimation and timely delivery of product increments

4. Transparency reduces non-detection risk

The Scrum principle of transparency around which the framework is built ensures that risks are detected and communicated early, leading to better risk handling and mitigation. Moreover, when conducting Scrum of Scrums Meetings, Impediments that one team is currently facing may be deemed a risk for other Scrum Teams in the future. This should be recognized in the Updated Impediments Log.

5. Iterative delivery reduces investment risk

Continuous delivery of value throughout the Scrum project lifecycle, as potentially shippable Deliverables are created after every Sprint, reduces investment risk for the customer.

Let me explain by giving few reasons for Why Scrum Always Works:

1) Communication shouldn't be the barrier.

Communication among the members of the team and the clients is what gets appreciated and promoted by Scrum, which results in attitude good for the team.

2) Amazingly Fast Results.

Getting the results after every few steps is what needed to get the feedback from the client, which works so good and helpful to work efficiently in the project.

3) Stay focused.

Time waste is just not the focus in this methodology as everything gets prioritised based on the importance of the item.

4) Estimates the reasonable time.

Production team's involvement makes it easier and fair to estimate the accurate time needed.

5) Organized on own.

One of the jobs of the production team is to make sure to achieve the specified goal on desired time. A combination of skill sets and skill levels are often best to promote a continuous work flow.

6) Open.

Scrum is always transparent: From the beginning, the client knows on what he could expect at the end of each step as he is the hand behind the product backlog. Within the team also they maintain equal transparency, in fact they main it throughout the project.

Chapter 20

Scrum Effort Estimation and Story Points

What is the best way for project managers to budget and allocate the time team members have to spend on a project? Depending on how the project will be managed-using traditional practices or agile management techniques, for example-determine whether capacity should be considered in terms of hours (time) or estimated difficulty (effort).

In traditional project management, managers estimate a team member's capacity for work based on task level planning. That is, they estimate how long they expect particular tasks will take to be completed and then assign tasks based on a team member's total available time using traditional tools like Gantt charts.

The problem with this approach is that it may lend itself to managing at the team member level, not the project level. That is, the project manager may end up focusing too much on keeping people busy and micromanaging individual workloads, rather than the overall success of the project being developed and the value it generates for the customer.

In complex new project development, like software teams, effort estimation utilizing story points may be a better answer than managing tasks.

How does this process of estimation work?

In a meeting during which the boss/project manager is absent, teams estimate in abstracted figures to quantify the relative effort associated with a particular story (a story is often composed of multiple tasks). Some teams use numeric sizing (i.e. a scale of 1 to 10) to estimate the "size" of a story, while others use t-shirt sizes (XS, S, M, L, XL, XXL, XXXL).

Some use the Fibonacci sequence (1, 2, 3, 5, 8, 13, 21, 34, etc.) to capture how difficulty tends to increase exponentially. Other teams have used dog breeds for estimation purposes, in which, say, a teacup poodle or Chihuahua would represent the smallest stories and a Great Dane or Bull Mastiff would represent the largest.

What's important for effort estimation is that the team shares an understanding of the scale it is using, so that everyone feels comfortable with the values of the scale.

Although the project manager (or Product Owner, in Scrum) needs these estimates to effectively prioritize backlog items and, consequently, forecast the delivery of the product to be developed based on velocity, only the team can make these estimates and the presence of the project manager/Product Owner could pressure (intentionally or otherwise) a team to minimize its effort estimates.

Even when team members estimate amongst themselves, it is recommended that everyone reveal their estimate at the same time to avoid influencing others. This process resembles a game of poker in that individuals "show their hands"-or reveal their estimates-simultaneously.

Traditional project managers may be uncomfortable with an approach to management that does not deal with the exactitude of budgeting hours for tasks.

But agile project management methods such as Scrum actually help managers focus on what really matters in development: the successful completion of the project and a customer who loves the product your team developed.

Chapter 21

Who Is A Scrum Master?

The Scrum Master is often looked up as a coach of the team who is relentlessly guiding, nurturing the team members in achieving its objective. He would go all out to ensure that the team performs at its peak potential. The Scrum Master usually is a former project manager or a technical team member but not restricted to them.

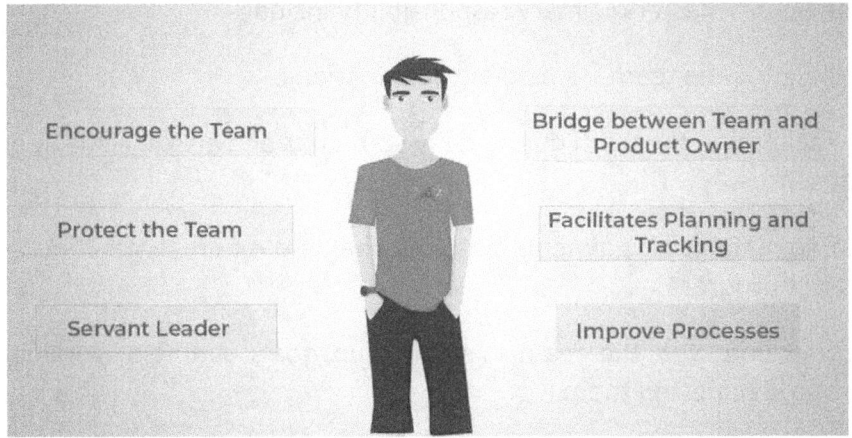

Encourage the Team

Bridge between Team and Product Owner

Protect the Team

Facilitates Planning and Tracking

Servant Leader

Improve Processes

HE may work with a single team or multiple teams at a given point in time.

The role of a Scrum Master is well defined in Scrum, also there is specialty training provided by the Scrum community. His Role need not be a full time job for a particular team. He may have other duties and responsibilities and would be playing the role of a Scrum Master on a part time basis.

During Scrum adoption the help of an external consultant can be sought until Scrum is fully mastered. An ideal character of a S.M is that he should be proactive and not reactive.

During the daily stand up the Scrum Master asks the team members the following 3 questions:

1. What did you do yesterday?

2. What will you do today?

3. Are there any impediments in your way?

Please note that he is not the project leader and cannot be held accountable for the outcome of the project.

The Scrum Masters primary responsibility includes:

1. Isolating the team from outside distractions.

2. Facilitating the team during daily stand ups and also in achieving consensus.

3. Eliminating impediments both internal and external affecting a team's progress.

4. Working with the team in setting up goals and also working towards achieving them.

5. Maintain a balance between the team and key stake holders of the project.

6. Facilitate meetings.

7. Works with the product owner in maintaining the product backlog.

8. Protects the team from external stakeholders and internally also ensures that the team is not complacent.

9. He also works with the technical team to implement technical practices required at the end of each sprint.

10. He ensures that the team members are accountable for the commitments they make.

11. Building the Release Plan.

12. Building the Scrum/Iteration plan.

Scrum Masters checklist includes the following:

1. How Is My Product Owner Doing?

2. How Is My Team Doing?

3. How are our engineering practices doing?

4. How is the organization doing?

A classic example to illustrate the role of a Scrum Master is that of a personal trainer in a gym. The personal trainer works in conjunction with the client in setting up goals, motivating and guiding him in achieving those goals.

The Scrum Master has an authority given to him by the team which he can exercise in case something goes wrong. Since the Scrum Master has limited authority his role is more difficult than that of a project manager.

Some Common Problems That A Scrum Master Faces

The Scrum Master has the primary role of facilitating this work strategy and ensuring that there is no impediment in the team's efforts at achieving their sprint target.

However, small glitches and unexpected errors always occur, and some are so common that all scrum masters should have some prepared or prospective solutions ready for them. It is not only time-saving and efficient, but also allows for the sharpening of one's crisis management abilities in the long run.

One of the most common problems that occur is that the product owner is unable to give the team the product backlog in time. Not knowing the priorities of the product owner, it is difficult for a development team to go forth in action.

In such a scenario, the scrum master can choose from among various options, depending upon the exact circumstances. Either the entire team could be allowed to take a break from sprinting, especially if the delay is supposed to be by a day or two.

On the other hand, a development team could also carry on with its planning meetings without giving priority to backlog, especially if the team has already completed some successful sprints.

The team can then create a rough draft of priorities if they are familiar with the general direction the product is taking and present it to the Product Owner for approval or amendment. Also, the team could take this break as an opportunity to review their work and gather feedback in order to further improve the scrum process.

Another issue which is fairly common, especially in MNC's where a great amount of work is conducted overseas, is that strict time boxed sprints are not maintained. However, to ensure that the scrum pattern is followed, a strict policy should be followed wherein such breach of procedure is unacceptable. If extreme situations are faced, the sprint completion can work upon a model of incentives as well.

Also, in most scenarios, overseas units are usually unaware of Scrum and how it works. Therefore, proper training, albeit a concise, short one must be conducted for otherwise the sailing shall not be smooth.

Many scrum masters also grapple with the question of whether it shall be better for an entire development team work on a particular aspect, complete the corresponding sprint and move on to the next, or the team be divided with various different groups handing different aspects at the same time.

The solution to this dilemma is dependent on various factors such as size of the team, the time constraints, the nature of the project, and so on and so forth. Often a master may choose to try both the techniques before selecting one as the standard, or choose not to have a standard method at all.

An experienced scrum master usually does has several such solutions at hand to deal with such hindrances. However, being prepared in advance is always best, for it displays foresight and efficiency that are both extremely crucial for business matters.

How to Choose a Scrum Master?

In their capacity as scrum master, one's duty is to guide, oversee and facilitate that the scrum work process is unimpeded, and used optimally to ensure higher efficiency in product development projects.

However, for scrum to be successful, it is extremely important that all those invested in it, be it the Scrum Master, Product Owner or Development Team, understand the nature of their responsibilities and therefore do what is expected of them, which will not be possible until and unless, all these roles are well-understood by those assigned to them.

Often, when a sudden switch is made from other agile strategies to scrum, there may be some difficulties in appointing the scrum master, for it is an important post that must be filled by exactly the right candidate.

The position may be designated either by the work team itself, or chosen by senior management that is not involved in the everyday working of these projects. The question is, how should the decision about the appointment of the scrum master be made?

The answer lies in understanding the nature of work that being a scrum master entails, and which kind of person shall be suitable for it. The person appointed for this job is typically associated with servant-leader qualities, which implies that he maintains a balance between leading the team, and working for it to ensure that there are no obstacles in its working process.

While he is definitely a figure of authority, the master should recognize that the final decision regarding the product development strategy within scrum is that of the development team; he should only have an advisory role in that capacity.

Majority of his work is to plan and schedule meetings, establish communication between the product owner and development team and protect the latter from facing distractions of any kind. Therefore, the master should be a person of experience that has superior managerial skills, and crisis management abilities.

It is often assumed that the position of scrum master is similar to that of a project manager, and thus, if the previous arrangement was such, he/she can be appointed into this new office.

However, it is important to remember that a project manager works in a more authoritative capacity where final approval for everything is in his hands. Since, the scenario is not quite as similar in the case of the latter, often a problem may arise if the project manager is unable to understand the nature of change that it imbues.

Some teams also follow a system where the master is continually rotated, possible with different projects or different product owners. Most people believe that this is not a very sound system, because constant change in leadership allows for different outcome each time over.

Such a system shall be beneficial only when the team is looking to create learning opportunities, and wishes to educate all team members being in such a position, before deciding upon who shall be best for a long-term arrangement.

Chapter 22

Who Is A Good Scrum Master?

A scrum master is an irreplaceable member of the development process who provides an effective adoption of the agile software development methodology. This person can be called the inter link between marketing and development departments.

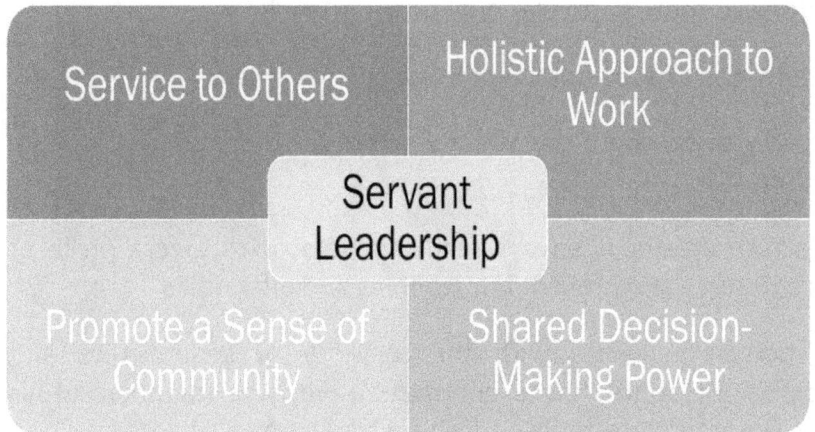

An inevitable part of everyday life of the team members are the stand-up meetings. They take place every day with the aim of keeping the stakeholders informed about the status of the development and testing procedures.

What Are the Core Aspects of the Daily Meeting?

• The scope of work what has already be done.

• The work plan for a day.

• The possible difficulties.

The discussion of these factors helps to realize the real state of affairs and to define further actions and steps of the development process. The exchange of information may prevent the occurrence of problems.

The communication should be effective on every stage of software development life cycle. For example, it is impossible to perform usability testing or functional testing of a high quality without sharing the obtained results and known facts. The same situation is with the development procedure.

The scrum master enables the team to work as a single entity. It is rather difficult to become a really good scrum master. This person should have some particular qualities.

What Are the Characteristics of a Good Scrum Master?

He is able to promote the effective work of the team and each its member.

The scrum master is always ready to help or to give a piece of advice to solve and prevent any troubles and difficulties.

This person is aware with the majority of scrum rules and principles. He shares these information with the members of his team. The scrum master is a coach for the team.

The master is a wise time planner. He is able to determine an approximate time needed for solving this or that problem.

He is the source of inspiration for the team. The scrum master knows how to motivate the specialists and how to raise the team spirit.

The scrum master never over controls the team.

The team leads, project managers, QA leads should keep these mentioned characteristics in mind. These items can be used not only during the development procedure, but also during mobile testing or desktop testing.

To perform mobile testing, desktop testing or web site testing efficiently these methods should be adjusted for each company and each project.

In agile software development, the Scrum Master role is a demanding part to play and requires a particular personality to do so effectively. Typically, the best Scrum Masters must be true team players, who find the accomplishments of others as gratifying as their own and can comfortably relinquish control to the Product Owner and team.

As such, traditional project managers seldom make successful Scrum Masters because Scrum demands that they resist the temptation to micro-manage the development team.

So what does a Scrum Master's work with an agile software development team look like? The primary function is to remove any barriers (or "impediments") that stand in the way of sprint goals. Put another way, the Scrum Master does everything within his or her power to facilitate productivity. If a developer's computer breaks, it's the job of the Scrum Master to fix it or replace it.

If a team room is too hot, it's the Scrum Master's task to cool it down and create a comfortable environment where developers remain focused on their work. It's easy to sum up the work a Scrum Master does in a sentence, but that hardly accounts for the infinite number of scenarios he or she might encounter while serving a development team.

But a Scrum Master's work isn't just limited to the team; he or she also has a responsibility to help the Product Owner maximize productivity. This might include helping to maintain the backlog and release plan or it might entail radiating Scrum artifacts - such as burndown charts - to ensure the Product Owner is apprised of the team's successes.

Using Scrum to manage agile software development is the leading strategy to help teams reduce risk and associated costs, while increasing the quality of a team's releases. Through an emphasis on communication and collaboration, Scrum brings everyone together - from developers to stakeholders - to build a better product.

Chapter 23

Ways a Scrum Master Improves a Software Development Team's Performance

A highly collaborative and well-managed scrum team is ideal for agile software development. With values like: courage, openness, commitment, and respect, these scrum teams feature a more collaborative and transparent management style organized to best complete the tasks at hand.

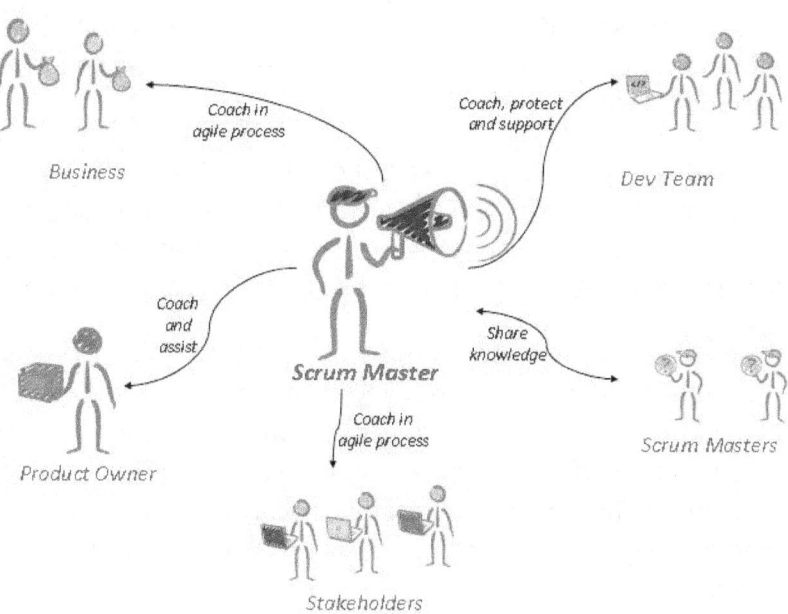

A scrum team consists of different roles which all work together to create a new product from start to finish. The scrum master is the person designated to keep group members focused on the project.

The short sprint style, in which this software development methodology organizes and completes work, requires a scrum master to coach and push the team forward.

Because a scrum master is essential to an agile team, their role has many different obligations. They are often expected to provide a clear and coherent vision of the project, ongoing support and organization, clear documentation, and much more.

There are several ways that the scrum master is able to improve overall performance, while maintaining structure. Here are four of them:

Strengthens Agility: Scrum teams need to be able to shape-shift and go with the project flow. Agile development came about in part as a response to deficiencies in the waterfall method. Software development with scrum focuses on the collaboration and organization of the entire team.

As the leader of the team, the scrum master is tasked with helping the team work together while allowing for flexibility. Becoming agile and adaptable only improves the team's ability to work with all of the issues that may arise over the course of a typical project.

Increases Velocity: As a scrum master, it is your job to keep the software development team moving forward even with setbacks. Scrum masters work hard to encourage and support team members in their effort to deliver high quality results as efficiently as possible. This involves careful documentation, managing stakeholder expectations, providing realistic time estimates, and much more.

Improves Communication: A scrum team is known for its collaborative approach to software development. Communication is at the heart of this collaboration. Daily scrum meetings are a great way to improve the team's success. This meeting is typically brief but also extremely informative and helpful. Ongoing communication throughout the project is a trait all effective scrum masters share.

Builds up Morale: A scrum master has a very important perspective on the team, focusing more globally on all the people involved on the project. Working together in a close-knit style, it's necessary for the team to not only get a long, but to ideally develop trust and friendships.

Creating an open environment where people feel valued is extremely important for the team. Even when things are going smoothly, it's important to continually strive to improve morale, encouraging team members to support one another and to effectively work through conflict, if it arises.

While a scrum master may not be directly involved in coding software, user experience design, or QA testing, their role on an agile team is extremely important. Not only do they tend to understand the more granular day-to-day work expectations, but they also have the bigger aerial view of the project and all of the people involved.

While the scrum master may be the main leader of the team, other team members are encouraged to take responsibility and initiative for their work. Many have found that this collaborative and organized approach to software development offers the best in terms of leadership and project management.

Chapter 24

Retrospection And Reworking Tool For A Scrum Master

Many experts believe that a process of retrospection and reworking is a key step towards facilitating the same. The role of the Scrum Master in allowing for such innovative techniques for the betterment of Scrum becomes highly significant.

The Scrum Master has a unique nature of "servant-leader" responsibility, and thus, ensuring that the work strategy is always at its optimal functionality, falls within the purview of his duty.

A Typical Sprint Retrospective Model

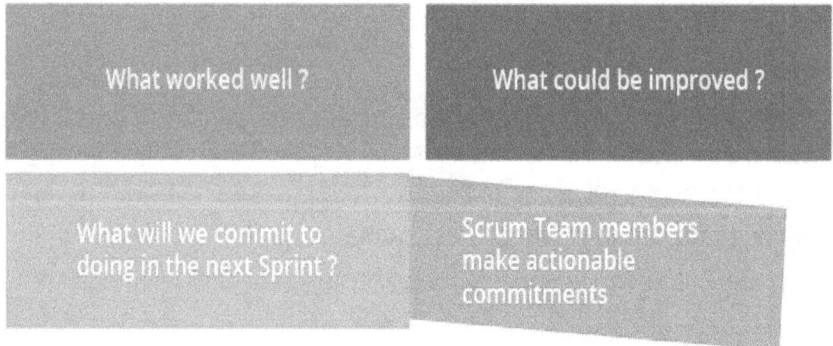

Calling for periodic meetings for retrospection and reworking can be very beneficial in increasing the productive potentiality of Scrum. Such meetings can be extremely helpful, especially if the Development Team takes it seriously, not deeming it a useless formality, but an effective method of affecting change.

There are certain ways in which a Scrum Master can orient a review meeting such that is bears conclusive results. It can begin with the Development Team members opining on what mechanisms bore best results in the previous sprint; they can put forth a personal as well as team perspective.

Keeping these strengths of the system in mind, they can reach a consensus over what aspects of the work model were beneficial for all. This should be followed by pinpointing the weaknesses.

There's a simple exercise for doing the same--all team members should be asked to articulate what they would have changed in the hypothetical scenario that the previous sprint was to be redone. An individual opinion should be obtained from each member, and the results must be displayed for all to see.

A discussion of these weaknesses should aim at finding alternative approaches, and all possible solutions should be put up to vote. In this manner, the team itself shall confront and realize its own merits and weaknesses, though in an inclusive, democratic manner.

It is important to realize that the initiative of the Scrum Master alone cannot bear results. If proper retrospection and reworking is to be enabled, the team members need to be vocal and expressive, with a strong commitment to the idea of making improvements to Scrum.

It is therefore important that individual opinions be invited such that there is no room for anyone to abstain from putting forth their opinion. Since, it is not uncommon that teams find such meetings utterly ineffective, it is the Scrum Master's leadership and managerial qualities that become highly significant here.

When conducting these sessions of retrospection, the focus should not be on how much output was produced or not produced, it should be to pinpoint where the Scrum strategy faltered, where the work process was lacking or inadequate.

Enhancing productivity is not the explicit but implicit aim of such retrospection; the primary objective is to somehow enhance the strategic nuances of the working process.

Chapter 25

Scrum Software Development And Outsourcing

The scrum development method is based on working in sprints, which are short periods of time in which the team is able to produce incremental project deliverables.

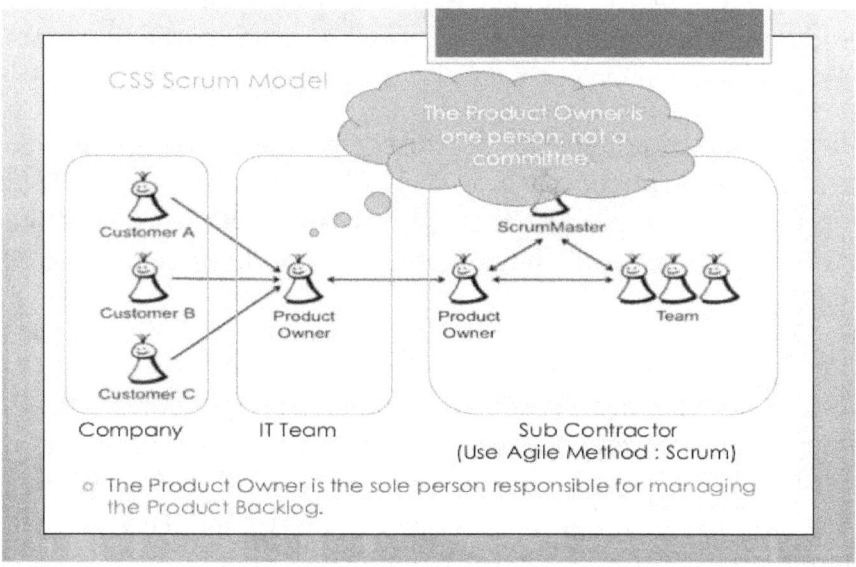

The Scrum methodology utilizes three main roles, the ScrumMaster, who facilitates the group, the Product Owner, who represents the business unit that will use the software and the Team, made up of software developers.

Before each sprint, there is a planning meeting with the entire group involved in the project in order to review what was accomplished in the previous sprint and what will be accomplished in the next.

Each sprint has a specific timeframe and if all the work is not finished, it goes into the "backlog" where the group can pull requirements for future sprints. The team has short daily meetings called "stand-ups" to discuss the project and how each person is progressing and identify any impediments to progress.

The scrum methodology has many advantages, including flexibility. The product owner does not need to know all the requirements in the beginning of development and any new technology developed can be incorporated into the new product.

If one aspect of the product is not working or is not what the product owner had in mind, it can be easily changed before anything is permanent.

The product owner is involved in the entire development process so he or she can continuously provide feedback and reduce the risk of ending up with a product that is not useable. Also, because the team meets daily, anything that is not working is discovered quickly.

The Scrum development methodology can work well with an outsourced team even though it depends on regular meetings. In order for the methodology to work though, the team must meet on a daily basis. When two groups are working in different countries, daily "scrums" (stand-ups) allow them to stay on-task and engaged with the work of the off-site team members.

Many groups make the off-site team seem closer through the use of video. The meetings go more smoothly when the team is working in the same or similar time zones. Nearshoring, or outsourcing to a country close to the company's county of origin, is ideal since it cuts down on language barriers and cultural differences, allowing the team to work well together.

The similar time zone is also a key factor for success. If the off-site team is working at the same time as the base team, they can join stand-ups and ad hoc meetings and ask questions throughout the day.

In traditional software development methodologies, the product requirements are given to the outsourced team at the beginning of the project; the overseas team produces a product and demonstrates a completed product at the end.

There is a lack of communication between product owner, the development company and the outsourced team. There could be many misunderstandings between the groups. The Scrum methodology cuts down on those misunderstandings between teams in different countries.

The Scrum software development methodology has many advantages over the traditional software development methods. Overall, it reduces the risk of producing an unusable product.

The frequent meetings keep the development team working closely together even if they are not geographically close together. Scrum is a great methodology for working with a nearshore product development partner

Chapter 26

Pitfalls To Avoid When Implementing Scrum

Scrum, having its roots in Agile methodology, can be effectively employed for almost any type of project. However, scrum is most preferred for software development purposes. The scrum process is ideally suited for rapidly changing project environments.

Scrum Master and Product Owner Functions Scale Differently

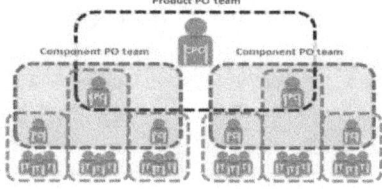

It is most useful, and its potential can be tapped in the best manner, when the user related requirements are changed frequently, or randomly, due to various reasons. The methodology makes it possible to incorporate the changes easily and effectively within its development cycle, and still generate positive outputs.

The true essence and working of scrum

According to scrum methodology, development occurs in short bursts of activity known as "sprints". Each sprint can generally last from two to four weeks.

Each sprint begins with a meeting, known as a "sprint meeting", and typically concludes with clearly defined and set out development objectives. Sprint meetings are very brief, and occur daily before the commencement of the sprint for that particular day.

The main objective of the meeting is to apprise everyone about how much development progress has been made since the previous day, and what objectives are to be achieved on the particular working day.

The main purpose of scrum is to aid the team members in inspecting and adapting to the changes, and providing transparency with regards the working of the project.

Another main advantage offered by scrum framework is to increase the involvement, and the interaction of the client with the team members.

The client remains apprised about the most recent development status, which helps him or her to undertake informed decisions about what further development activities are required to complete the project in totality, and what features and functionalities need to be omitted, or which have become redundant during the development cycle.

Pitfalls while implementing scrum

Scrum is a framework, a methodology based upon an organized thought process developed specially to cater to changing development requirements, and the main issue with Agile and scrum is that the methodology is to be implemented, or its rules enforced in a proper manner.

Many a times, when organizations are not properly trained in the implementation of the methodology, there is a tendency to fall back upon old development methods, consciously or unconsciously, thus making scrum redundant.

Traditional development methods such as Waterfall have been in existence since a long time, and people are more familiar with them. Project managers have practiced these methods for a long time, and they are more conversant with them.

Scrum can be difficult to implement, and if the manager is not properly trained, he or she may substitute some of the scrum related processes with Waterfall methods.

The objective is to provide a specific solution during the development cycle, and when the person fails to implement scrum in a particular development related process, he or she "patches" up scrum implementation process with a Waterfall technique. This should be avoided at all costs. Scrum should be implemented in totality for it to be effective.

Chapter 27

Scrum Vs Extreme Programming

The Agile Process or software development refers to a set of software development methods which are based on iterative development. In this process, the solutions and requirements both evolve mutual collaboration between cross functional teams. These teams are self-organizing in nature.

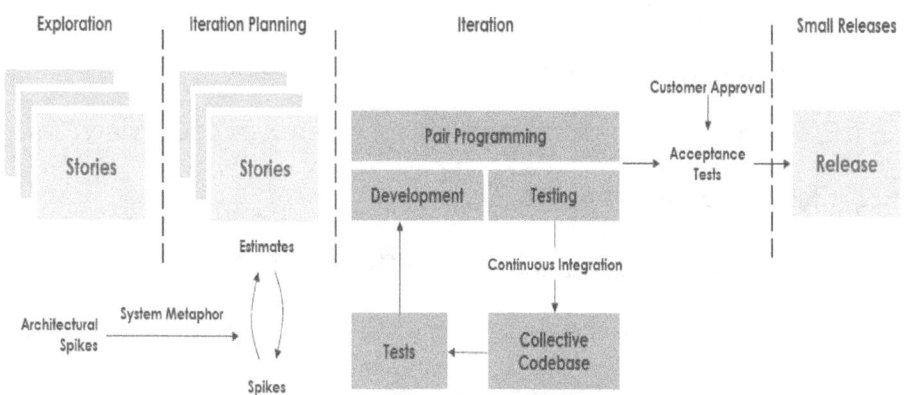

The Agile software development approach usually promotes a regimented kind of project management process which encourages:

1. Frequent adaptation and inspection

2. Self-organization and accountability

3. A leadership philosophy which promotes teamwork

4. A business approach which bring into line the development with customer needs and company goals

5. And a group of best engineering practices having an intention to allow for rapid delivery of good-quality software.

Extreme Programming (EP)

It is a software development methodology with an intention to enhance software responsiveness and quality to the volatile requirements of customers. Being a type of Agile process, it promotes frequent releases in small development cycles. This introduces checkpoints and improves the productivity in a way that the new requirements from customers can be adopted.

The advantages of Extreme Programming are:

1. Unit testing of all code

2. Avoiding programming of features until needed

3. Programming in pairs or carrying out extensive code review

4. Clarity and simplicity in code

5. Volatile customer requirements better understood

6. A flag management structure

7. Frequent communication between the programmers and even with the customer

The drawbacks of Extreme programming are:

1. No documented compromises of user conflicts

2. Unstable requirements

3. Lack of overall design document or specification

4. Incorporates inadequate software design

5. Necessitates meetings at recurrent intervals at huge expense to customers

6. Can enlarge the risk of scope creep due to the lack of thorough requirements documentation

7. Requires excess of cultural change to adopt

Scrum

Scrum is an incremental, iterative framework for agile software development and project management. The word "Scrum" is not really an acronym. However, many companies using this methodology spell it with capital letters.

Initially Scrum methodology was focused for management of software development projects, but in recent times it can be used to run general program/project management approach or software maintenance teams. Scrum, which contains sets of predefined roles and practices, is a process skeleton. Main roles in this method are:

1. Product Owner - Represents Stakeholders

2. Scrum Master - The one responsible for maintaining the processes

3. Team - A cross functional group of about 6-8 people who do actual design, testing, implementation, etc.

Each of the iteration is called a "sprint", typical time frame for which is normally about two to four weeks. The length of each sprint is decided by the team. The product "backlog" pushes the set of features into a spring. These features are prioritized set of higher level requirements for the task to be carried out.

Based on this product "backlog", the team determines how many of the items can be completed in the next sprint. Once the sprint begins, nobody is allowed to alter the sprint backlog, which means that the set of requirements are frozen. On successful completion of a sprint, the team demonstrates the usage of that particular software.

This methodology should be encouraged in organizations since the major advantage of using the Scrum is that it enables the creation of teams which are highly self-organizing in nature. This is achieved by encouraging verbal communication amongst the team members, co-location of all the team members and disciplines which are involved for the project.

Differences between Scrum and Extreme Programming(EP):

1. The time span for iterative sprints is different in both approaches.

2. Changes are not allowed by the Scrum teams during their sprints. Whereas Extreme Programming teams have to be much more agreeable to changes.

3. Work is done by EP teams in strict priority order. Whereas in case of Scrum, the product owner prioritizes the set of activities.

4. EP does prescribe some engineering practices; Scrum does not.

Chapter 28

Enterprise Adaptation of the Scrum Framework

There are 3 basic fundamentals of Agile methodology or Scrum process are as followings:

Transparency - a great way of building this pillar is visualization. Common realization is that boards depict the workflow.

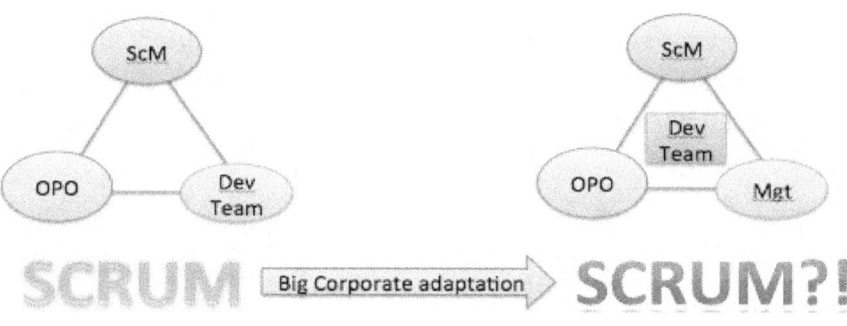

Monitor - one of the most important aspects of agile methodologies. It enables improvements every day. Through monitoring, we learn where we are now and discover what we need to do to make our vision and mission. Common realization is measuring velocity, feedback through demonstrations and retrospectives.

Fast Forward - establishes micro planning which implements a culture to do the most important thing first. Through micro planning, we merge changes fast and alternative progress path when obstacles are found. One of the key approaches to mitigate risks is by distributing risk elements into smaller timeframes.

The enterprise wanted a management upgrade. Agile was the new buzz so we decided to transform into agile management. We had decided to carry out Scrum.

To complete our agile transformation, we have applied all 3 fundamentals of agile methodology stated above. So, we have now transformed our organization and become agile, right? Let's dig a little deeper into that.

Agile is a methodology for a way of working and be effective in R&D development. Orchestration is necessary between development team and many other existing roles to gain success.

For management, agile transformation is not only about changing some methods of working, the transformation is also about mindset changes, so it is as much as a philosophy as it is a methodology.

One hidden philosophy of agile is control. In agile management, the control is given to agile teams, meaning ideally no external control shall be necessary. A methodology that may transformation the enterprise from traditional management towards agile leadership.

Traditionally, hierarchical management is responsible for control and governance of that enterprise.

Does that mean the management is obsolete in agile methodology?

How do you keep all the managers in the organization as Scrum framework doesn't define the manager role?

The easier way to answer this question was to change the Scrum framework. The enterprise themselves made all adaptation and enforced into practice. There was no standard adaptation of the methodology.

Scrum is a very light weight framework that tries to give a guideline for value driven software development. It is very difficult, close to impossible to define a framework that fits all needs. Implementation of Scrum framework in enterprises shall require tailoring.

The company's culture and existing leadership style will always influence the adaptation process. One key point is that when every enterprise makes its own version of Scrum, we may lose the founding philosophy of Agile. For long-term benefits, we shall strive to find some common elements and try to standardize the adaptation as much as possible.

Agile transformation and Scrum adaptation shall always emphasize our efforts to create self-organizing teams. Self-organizing teams are the primary lead to agile management culture in the enterprise

Chapter 29

Scrum Transitions

Transitioning to Scrum or any Agile framework is difficult and making sure that it is sustainable is key to its success. Many a coach or Agile firm do not see this or prefer not to see it. They see the revenue behind it more valuable to them then truly assisting a transformation.

Scrum Transition/Adoption Team

- Transition/Adoption requires organizational buy-in
- Create a cross-functional transition/adoption team
- Focus on the highest priority items and deliver results
- Create one month sprints with weekly Scrums

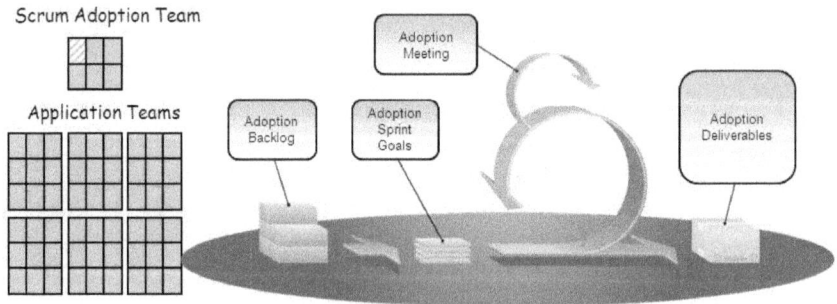

If an Agile firm is to help you transition to scrum they will identify the above scenarios as anti-patterns. Anti-Scrum patterns arise from only adopting what is convenient and keeping what is comfortable to you.

To adopt scrum you need to be open to transparency, commit to supporting your teams quest to self-organization, and be willing to get out of your comfort zone. Be ready to stay grounded despite project pressures. Understand the corporate culture will need to change and set a strategy in place to embed agile in the culture.

If your agile transition is to last, make sure it is sustainable. Understand and communicate upfront what limitations your team will have. Set boundaries early, self-organization does not mean they do whatever they want. Keep in mind the other organization's process improvement models (CMMI) or regulatory requirements unless you can move away from them.

Be sure to include how the team will interact with other departments. Identify any external dependencies and establish a solution early on. Set the organizational goals in transitioning and communicate them with everyone.

The goals should be made from a business perspective. What is your organization's business needs and how can they be met? If the business needs are to increase speed to market, how will you meet them without impacting quality? Agile is all about your end user, whether it is another department or customer.

What To Consider When Transitioning To Scrum:

If you are contemplating transitioning to Agile or Scrum you need to know consider a few things before you get started. Transitioning to scrum no matter the size of the organization is no easy task. So here are three things to consider before diving in.

One:

Understand what you are getting into. I have coached individuals who want to move the organization to Scrum and Agile but don't really understand what it means. This is a recipe for disaster. When I describe Agile to students, I describe it as a state of mind.

But this state of mind is difficult for some, and while transitioning to scrum is trendy, it is not a good reason to take your team through it. Ask yourself do you know what it means to be Agile! Can you adopt the agile principles and values (Respect, Focus, Commit, Courage, and Openness).

Agile is a philosophy. One which believes code should be worked iteratively and incrementally. Where business requirements are not written all upfront. Would you be willing to forgo BRD's? Would you be willing to empower your team?

Two:

Still interested in transitioning to agile or scrum? Then you need to consider getting a Scrum coach. This individual will help you through the transition. They should ask you a lot of tough questions to help you get there. Outline your goals and walk them through it.

Make sure your goals agree with the reason you choose to transition? If they don't, go back and review. The Coach will help keep you in check and help teams keep these goals in mind. They will identify scrum anti-patterns and give you suggestions on how to correct these patterns. They help grow your teams and look to keeping an agile environment.

Three:

Now that you have your scrum coach engage other departmental managers that are necessary for the success of your teams. Make an agreement with these other line managers upfront that will cover approvals that may be required, change in process that may need to be made. Have your Scrum Coach document this engagement model to communicate it to all involved.

Chapter 30

Being An Effective Scrum Master

A Scrum master is like a leg in the tripod of the Scrum team, with the other two being the product owner and the development team. The relationship of the product owner with the business representative is balanced out by the Scrum master's relationship with the development team.

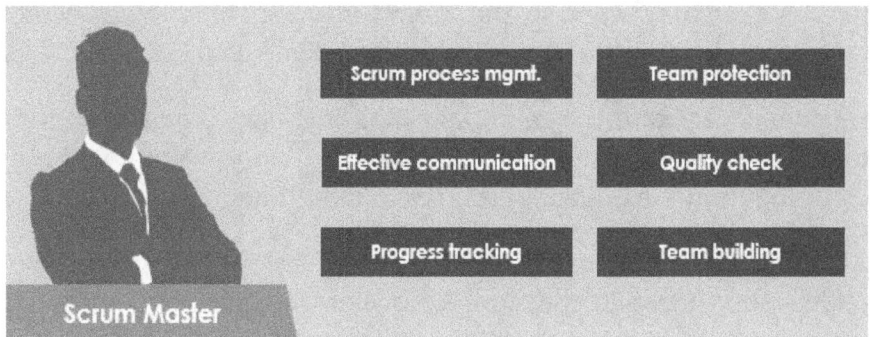

His role is to support the team in becoming self-organized, to remove any obstacles the team might be facing and to ensure that the Scrum methodology is being followed. However, unlike the product owner, he not play a management or supervisory role for the team.

The first step to being an effective Scrum master is to understand the principles of Scrum extremely well. As a part of this, he should be well aware of what Scrum can and cannot achieve. He must ensure that daily Scrum meetings are held and other important processes of Scrum are followed and that the team does not veer off course.

It is important that a Scrum master knows how to use different tools and techniques such as tracking and value of metrics, and should have knowledge of software development process and other agile methodologies. What is even more important to become an effective Scrum master is to hone soft skills such as leadership and determination.

Adopting Scrum, especially when the team is not exposed to Scrum, can be challenging, and the change can sometimes be met with resistance. He will have to work with a lot of perseverance to overcome this and help create an atmosphere in which team members will stand behind Scrum.

He can assists the team by addressing any issues or removing any hurdles that may stand in the team's way. Possible issues could range from personality conflict to product ownership.

He should facilitate the team, allowing it to self-organize and to determine the best way to deliver high value without compromising the ever-important Scrum methodology.

An effective Scrum master will strive to establish an amicable relationship between the product owner and team members. A product owner might at times be controlling and demanding.

It is the Scrum master's responsibility to be the pacifier and help the team maintain its morale and communicate effectively with the product owner to resolve any issues.

An important aspect of agile is that it places "individuals and interactions over processes and tools." An effective Scrum Master acts as a servant-leader. When managing the team, he does not direct the team but leads by example and also serves it by removing any impediments and allowing it to decide the best way to grow and perform.

Being a servant-leader also means that he re-communicates the project vision to ensure the team is heading in the right direction. As a leader, it is also his responsibility to encourage the team by offerings rewards to keep the team motivated to continuously improve.

Only the most knowledgeable and accomplished scrum master can play his role properly between the team and the project designers; as it is not a very easy position. There is no way a sloppy person can succeed in this capacity of scrum team manager.

Again the stakeholders are the customers, and their views must not be shunted aside. On the other hand, they must not be too overbearing with the risk that they might interfere with the decisions made at scrum meetings.

The role of this person is to evaluate everything and keep all the players in a well- balanced working relationship. He must ward off unnecessary interference but also express the sentiments of the product developers to the scrum team.

The Scrum Master must be able to absorb all the details of the project plan. He does this in order to interpret it to the team at the scrum meetings by introducing discussions at the very onset of the work.

The leader acts as the important link for the team and the management. Knowing the urgency and the voracious nature of the scrum sprints, this person must do everything to protect the team from unwarranted disruptions.

Such interference may occur as a result of overzealous CEO Stakeholders or the management. For example, some of them tend to try to introduce completely new stuff that was never considered in the original picture of things. If this is allowed to go on, the time frames for the completion of the project and the estimates or costs may be negatively affected.

The Scrum Master must have the knack of picking out the right people for the team, those who are fully committed to the success of the scrum. This is because a poor quality worker lags behind at sprints and may lead to the production of substandard product.

This is why it is said the right leader is the one with great managerial qualities.

The scrum is managed by the Scrum Master who must deal with the various impediments that might occur, from time to time. He wants the team to achieve its set goals. He thrashes out the work for the team and enables them to move faster and accurately.

Sometimes the person is not the leader of the scrum but is the one who manages the process of production, so he manages the teams working on the project. He makes sure that the teams remain focused and able to deliver at all times. This is why it is true to describe the role of this person as the Scrum facilitator. He is the manager who is responsible for the whole production from the beginning to the end.

Conclusion

Scrum is a project management framework used to help project managers effectively complete heavy workloads or complicated projects.

It was initially created to be used solely within software development, but can be applied to any project involving complicated work. Despite the many different possibilities Scrum provides, the principal of the process is actually very simple.

Scrum was created in 1993 by Jeff Sutherland who had studied a Harvard Business Review piece by Takeuchi and Nonaka. The piece discussed comparisons between teams of high performance individuals and the rugby formation of a scrum. Sutherland borrowed the term to label his project management framework.

The methodology is used by leading corporations worldwide and exists to help absolutely anyone effectively approach a complex project. The processes within the system are agile and suitable for a broad spectrum of applications, which means its use is not restricted to software development.

The idea of the Scrum process is ensuring that no matter why the work has been stopped, the work that has been completed will be the most important when the project closes.

The beauty of the process is the fact that it can streamline many different types of project from many different industries. The majority of project management training courses will now discuss Scrum as an innovative agile framework which is used by more than half of companies using this type of process.

Some applications of Scrum are:

Universities - using the process to successfully deliver completed projects to important customers.

The Military - using the process to successfully plan and prepare ships for distribution.

Charities - using the process to quickly and effectively plan and create a charity event.

Due to its endless possibilities and potential for success, Scrum is becoming more and more popular with every industry and sector within the world of project management.

Agile project management is no longer reserved just for IT projects so if you are wondering whether agile project management is right for you just give it a try; it could be one of the factors that contribute to a successful project.

Finally, if you enjoyed this book, then I'd like to ask you for a favor, would you be kind enough to leave a review for this book on Amazon? It'd be greatly appreciated!

Leave a review for this book on Amazon!